I0137521

SOUL
CYPHERS

DECODING A

LIFE OF HOPE

& HAPPINESS

ROBERT CLANCY

SOUL
CYPHERS

DECODING A
LIFE OF HOPE
& HAPPINESS

By *Robert Clancy*

Foreword by Marci Shimoff

Mohawk Street Press
New York

FIRST EDITION

Library of Congress Cataloging-in-Publication Data
Clancy, Robert Steven

Soul Cyphers.
p.cm.

Summary: Soul Cyphers: Decoding a Life of Hope and Happiness is a
collection of inspirational stories and spiritual thoughts that guides one to
a path of healing, grace, peace, compassion, happiness,
and unconditional love.

[1. Self-Help – Inspirational 2. Memoir 3. Essays 4. Creative Nonfiction]

ISBN 978-0-9859395-3-3

For information about permission to reproduce selections
from this book, write:

Permissions, Guide to the Soul, 135 Mohawk Street, Cohoes, NY 12047
or email to permissions@guidetothesoul.com.

Cover, Layout & Design:
Neil Wright, Spiral Design Studio, LLC
(SpiralDesign.com)

The Mohawk Street Press logo is a trademark of Guide to the Soul, LLC.

All stories contained in this book are true. Some names, places, and other identifying details
have been changed to protect individual privacy.

DEDICATION

*This book is graciously dedicated in memory of
the following kindhearted souls:*

*Caitlin Clancy, Jeffrey Wayne Krauss and
Cindy Wachenheim*

*What happens in your life may be fated and
certainly cannot be changed. You can only
go forth with an angel's kiss upon your lips,
a Divine hand upon your heart and
God's grace within soul.*

For my beloved wife Lauren

For my son Sean, and extended family—
Ramona, Eugenio, and Marius

TABLE OF CONTENTS

PRAISE FOR SOUL CYPHERS

"I can't think of a better time for a book like *Soul Cyphers* to be birthed. These days, so many people feel like they're floundering and devoid of purpose. Many have even lost hope. But the truth is that we are all here for a reason. This book will help you align with your soul's destiny, a key to experiencing deep and lasting happiness."

—from foreword by **Marci Shimoff**, New York Times #1 bestselling author of *Chicken Soup for the Woman's Soul*

"A wonderful awakening for your soul! A brilliant light to guide you on your pathway through life, *Soul Cyphers* lifts you up, enlightens your day, and becomes your guide on an empowering journey to discover your self-worth...*priceless*.

—**Temple Hayes**, Difference-maker, Intl. Speaker; Author of *When Did You Die?*

"Robert Clancy has written a brilliant, uplifting book. It is the key to unlocking your highest potential and grace-filled purpose. *Soul Cyphers* is a beautiful guide for anyone seeking a more fulfilling life."

—**Robin Jay**, Award-winning filmmaker, *The Keeper of the Keys* and *The Secrets of the Keys*

"Enlightening is an understatement. Not since *The Shack* have I read such and engaging and compelling book to reaffirm my spiritual connection. Robert Clancy is a true angelic light in our world. His beautifully-written book, *Soul Cyphers*, decodes every aspect of your heart and dreams, while providing you with a spiritual guide to get you through even the darkest of days."

—**Teresa de Grosbois**, Four time international bestselling author

"Robert is one of a kind. He really knows people and how to help them. His message beautifully covers heath—whether physical, mental, or spiritual—as an important aspect of your well-being. I'm keeping this book by my bed and I suggest you do as well."

—**Mark Alyn**, Award-winning host and producer of *Late Night Health Radio*

"Beautifully written and deeply inspiring, Robert Clancy's book will ignite your heart to higher love and transform your moments into a series of miraculous awakenings."

—**Paul Samuel Dolman**, Host of *What Matters Most* and author of *Hitchhiking with Larry David: A True Story from Martha's Vineyard*

ACKNOWLEDGEMENTS

The path to *Soul Cyphers* was not created by pen to paper or keys typed into a screen, but by the many beautiful kind souls and kindred spirits I have met along my life's highway. Thank you for guiding me and keeping me on my true path.

My heartfelt gratitude goes out to all who helped make this book happen by contributing their inspirational stories for this book.

First, to my wife and life partner Lauren—you are the kindest heart I have ever known. My love for you only grows stronger each and every day.

Next, to my son Sean, you are my greatest gift. You've given me more than you'll ever know in this life and to my entire family, thank you for teaching me what love truly is.

To my extended family: my daughter Ramona and sons Eugenio and Marius. Thank you for coming into my life, sharing your hearts, and becoming part of our family. I look forward to seeing your journeys unfold.

To my dad, for being the ultimate volunteer by landing on Utah Beach during the D-Day invasion on June 6, 1944; and to my mom, who taught me the importance of community service and compassion for others.

To the Wachenheim family for showing me what true grace is.

To my team at Spiral Design Studio, for inspiring me every day through your incredible creativity.

To Dea Shandera-Hunter, Debra Poneman, Robin Jay and Swami Sadashiva Tirtha—you are amazing lights in our world.

To Teresa de Grosbois and the *Evolutionary Business Council* for your guidance, support and mentorship.

To Anna Pereira and Shari Alyse from *The Wellness Universe* for your community support and wonderful connections.

Finally, thank you to all of my friends, volunteers, and believers in love around the world. You've changed me in so many profound ways, I can't count them all.

CONTRIBUTORS
SPECIAL THANKS

I wish to extend a special thanks to the following beautiful souls who shared their inspiring stories with me for this book:

Scott Baker
In Scott's honor, please support the Leukemia & Lymphoma Society
http://www.lls.org

Mark Eder
In Mark's honor, please support the JDRF Diabetes Foundation of Northeastern NY
http://www.jdrf.org/neny/

Steve Lobel
In Steve's honor, please support the Phoenix Society
http://www.phoenix-society.org

Lee Lomas
In Lee's honor, please support TESSA
https://www.TESSAcs.org

Christine Powers
In Christine's honor, please support 350.org
https://350.org

The Wachenheim Family
In the Wachenheim family's honor, please support Postpartum Support International
http://www.postpartum.net

May your stories inspire others on their roads to healing and compassion.

FOREWORD

by Marci Shimoff

D o you ever wish you could reprogram yourself for a happier, more joy-filled, loving life? With the book you hold in your hands, you can do just that.

I was first introduced to Robert Clancy through a mutual friend who sent me some of Robert's beautiful writing. I was so moved by what I read, I decided that I had to learn more about him. The first time we spoke, I knew my intuition was correct: he is a bright light in our world, with great wisdom and love to share. In fact, I got "godbumps" when he told me about his message, his work and his vision for the world.

Robert life's purpose is to help people transform their unhappy or mediocre lives into lives that are not only happy, but miraculous. This is a mission that's very close to my own heart, and I'm delighted to support a kindred spirit in his mission to help people heal and thrive.

I can't think of a better time for a book like this to be birthed. These days, so many people feel like they're floundering and devoid of purpose. Many have even lost hope. But the truth is that we are all here for a reason. This book will help you align with your soul's destiny, a key to experiencing deep and lasting happiness.

And I have good news and bad news about happiness. I've spent two decades studying the science of happiness and have developed a body of knowledge about how to live in a state I call, "happy for no reason." This is an inner state of peace and well-being that doesn't depend on circumstances. The bad news is that most people have a negativity bias inherited from our caveman ancestors— giving us the tendency to notice and focus on the negatives in our lives. The good news is that we can rewire our brains by consciously retraining them to focus on and savor the positives. When we do this, we build new neural pathways that incline us toward more joy, love, and fulfillment.

In *Soul Cyphers*, Robert offers brilliant and powerful *life decodes* that allow for such transformation. He also includes moving stories to inspire you along with effective practices you can incorporate into your daily routine that are simple, yet life-changing.

I appreciate Robert's perspective that we are all connected to each other and to the essence of life, to a Divine Source. In reading this work, I am reminded of one of my favorite quotes from the classic Indian text, the Upanishads:

There is a light which shines beyond the world, beyond everything, beyond all, beyond the highest heaven. This is the light which shines within your heart.

Soul Cyphers captures the essence of that message. With this book, you'll find how bright your own light truly is. Enjoy your journey!

With love,

Marci Shimoff

#1 New York Times Bestselling Author, Happy for No Reason, Love For No Reason, Chicken Soup for the Woman's Soul

www.MarciShimoff.com
www.YourYearOfMiracles.com

INTRODUCTION

"Love has no end, because it's always writing the next beautiful chapter of your life."— Robert Clancy

○

O ur world is shifting at a dizzying pace, and most of us lack the tools to not only thrive, but even survive with their heart and soul intact. Technology whizzes by us, the increasingly complex global geopolitical landscape is incomprehensible, and displacement of all the "rules of life" that we have been clinging to can no longer move us into a place where we can flourish, no matter what is happening around us.

Soul Cyphers: Decoding a Life of Hope & Happiness guides you toward creating a joyful, balanced life. Universal themes of faith, hope, love, kindness, peace, compassion, forgiveness, and beauty are threaded throughout this book—uplifting you into a new state of being, where you can blossom and grow.

You whether you are old or young, poor or affluent, spiritual or not—are probably going through something challenging in your life right now. *Soul Cyphers* is written to support you in getting through these trying times. If you're dealing with loss (especially the death of a child), recovering from abuse, struggling with deep-rooted self-worth issues, or suffering from depression, I promise you that happiness is not an impossibility. Within this book, I unlock the keys and codes needed for shifting everything around you. And within you.

As a technology expert and professional programmer with a highly-developed spirituality, I view life in a way that most simply cannot. I *see* our world and life's mysteries as a puzzle, an algorithm, or a long line of code that needs cracking—a cypher if you will. More importantly, I know how to share what it is I see in a way through which you can benefit.

With the right tools, you can be empowered to "decode" the cyphers of your life, moving you into greater well-being and wholeness. This the essence of *Soul Cyphers*, and why I refer to the three exercises at the end of each chapter as *decodes*.

You have the power to turn yourself around and live a happier, more fulfilling life—you just need a little guidance, inspiration, and the example of someone who has done this very thing. *Soul Cyphers* offers the guidance you need, moving soulful stories from everyday people, inspirational quotes, enlightened teachings, and the inspiration that I've drawn from my life.

I was moved to write *Soul Cyphers* because of the responses I received from readers of my two previous books, audiences around the world that I have had the privilege to present to, and fans of my Facebook page. While they understood and enjoyed the general messages of my prior offerings, *they wanted to understand how to turn the inspiration they felt from my work and my presence into practical, long-lasting application in their everyday lives.* This book fulfills the longing that they—and countless others—share in seeking a pathway to action and tangible results.

Soul Cyphers is a steadfast companion as you embark down the path toward open-hearted, authentic, joyful living. I have turned my life around from despair and hopelessness, and have modeled this formula for you to do the same.

At age nineteen, I was at the lowest point of my life, and about six months from death. My life fell apart when several of my friends committed suicide or died in horrific car accidents. I gave up; I was lost. A friend reached out and taught me how to meditate. What transpired the first time I meditated is almost beyond belief. I was a few hours into this meditative state when a divine angelic messenger appeared. She greeted me with a kiss, and later touched my forehead with her index finger during the encounter. This touch opened the universe to my soul—I was plugged into all the knowledge and love in the universe. This angel not only healed me, she revealed what heaven is, what love is, and what my true life's path was. I was given a tremendous gift and responsibility. I am a highly technical and analytical person, yet I cannot deny what happened to me.

I held this divine encounter as a secret for nearly thirty years, telling only a handful of people because I was fearful of being judged. Some people will judge me, but I am resolved that I will not take this experience to my grave, and have included the full account in this book.

I know that your life began with love. All life begins with love. You can—and will—grow gracefully with every moment you share love, and ultimately when your life on this planet ends, your very essence becomes everything that love is.

Isn't it time you decode everything you are, leave behind everything you are not, and step into everything you are meant to be?

Wishing you much love & light!

/ Robert

THE MESSENGER

*"Faith, love, and death are all parts of life.
The differences among them are that faith carries us
through life, death ends our life, and love
transcends it."*— Robert Clancy

How would you change your life if you were shown proof of the Divine? How would you live the rest of your days? When I've thought deeply about the word *belief,* I discovered that everything about it is contained within the action of simply doing it—no proof. Your true faith is the one thing that allows you to unquestionably possess it.

For more than half my life, I've kept a secret from almost everyone who has known me—a deeply spiritual, life-changing encounter. When my mother passed away a few years ago, there was an additional layer of sadness because I never shared anything about this with her. I've kept this secret for two reasons: partially to avoid being judged and, to some extent, because it's been a gift I've held closely in my heart. Only God knows, with utter absolution, *the truth* of what I am about to share with you.

———⌖———

My sister was staring blankly at the floor with her hands folded. "You need to get some rest, Dad. You've been here all day and you haven't eaten anything. You need to be strong for Mom and for us. We'll keep watch over Mom. You've gotta get back to your room."

My father's good eye slowly peered over the rim of his glasses as he nodded in agreement.

My mother was losing her long battle with cancer and my family was holding vigil by her bedside at the nursing home. Both my parents lived at the same facility, but my father's room was on a different floor due to the additional care he required.

As my sister's voice died into the silence, no one seemed to know what to say, except me, yet I remained quiet. I was holding on to a secret, a profound secret that I desperately wanted to share with my father. I wanted him to know. I wanted everyone to know. I wanted them all to know that everything was going to be okay.

The ominous air in the room kept building until my sister leaned into me and prodded, "Bobby, can you take Dad up to his room? And make sure they get him something to eat. I'm really worried about him."

"I'm worried too," I admitted. "I can take him up."

Since suffering the stroke that paralyzed my father's left side, he'd been living at the nursing home. The impairment may have stolen his independence and compromised his speech, but it couldn't touch his fighting spirit. I've always thought of him as having a lion's heart. My father is a decorated, front-line combat medic who survived the D-Day invasion of Normandy and helped liberate a concentration camp during World War II. He knows more than most about how fragile and precious life is.

Still, I was worried that he might give up on life after my mother passed away. We all shared this concern. Earlier that year my parents celebrated sixty-four years of marriage. I couldn't imagine what it would be like to lose someone I've loved for that long, but I *knew* without a doubt that the love my parents shared would never die.

I grabbed the handles of my father's wheelchair and prayed, "Please let him believe me. Just let him *believe*." In that moment, I realized I had made the decision to tell him my secret.

The wheels of my dad's wheelchair creaked as I slowly pushed him down the hallway. Neither of us spoke a word until we reached the elevator.

As the elevator doors sealed us into privacy, I tilted my head down at him and said, "Mom is nearing the end. You understand this, right Dad?"

Pursing his lips, he nodded his head slowly in acknowledgment. There was no emotion on his eternally stoic face, but a shaky voice squeaked out of him, "Death and taxes... right?" One of my father's gifts has always been humor and even in this heart-breaking situation he managed to make me crack a small smile.

"Yep, Pop. The two things in life you can be sure of." *It was time to tell him there was something else I was sure of.*

The elevator doors shrugged open. The grin slowly drifted away from my face. I rolled him onto his floor, paused for a moment and knelt down next to him, "When we get to your room, is it all right if I sit with you for a little while?"

"Sure. What else are we gonna do?"

When we reached his room, I still contemplated not telling him the secret, but my soul spoke otherwise.

I perched myself hesitantly on the edge of his desk. "Dad... I have something to share with you and what I'm going to tell you is the God's honest truth. I'm not sure if you are going to believe me or not, but I pray that you do. I'm not sure where to begin, so I'm just going to tell you. I want you to know that there *is* another side—heaven is real. This I know without a shadow of doubt. Mom is going to be taken care of. In fact, we all are. When I was nineteen, an angel appeared to me—*a real angel*. I know it sounds crazy—when we die...well...it's not the end. The angel showed me what Heaven feels like and that our love and every act of kindness and compassion not only carry over with us, but they directly feed the universe now."

After revealing all this, I was suddenly back in that incredible moment of my life. It was a difficult and dark period for me. I'd broken up with my first serious girlfriend, and several friends had either committed suicide or were killed in a fatal car accident. I had given up on life and surrounded myself with negative people. *What's the point? We're all just gonna die anyway.*

I went out drinking almost every night of the week. I accepted rides from people who shouldn't have been on the road. I mixed a deadly cocktail of prescription drugs and alcohol to dull my inner pain. I didn't care. I felt so alone, and had no one to turn to for support—and I didn't want it. I was lost. If I had continued on this path, I would probably have been dead within six months to a year.

At that time I worked in a restaurant as a cashier and occasionally bartended. I was probably drinking more than I was serving. I was gaunt with dark circles under my eyes from the abuse I'd been doing to myself. The week I hit rock bottom, a waitress quietly pulled me aside at the end of my work shift. "I think you need help. Serious help. You're not looking so good."

At first, I shrugged her off. "No, I'm okay. I don't need any help."

She lowered her chin and her eyes pierced my soul. "I *know* what's going on with you."

I slowly placed my hand on my forehead as I noticed a tear rolling down my cheek. After a long pause, I tried again. "You're right. I don't know what to do with myself. I'm throwing my life away."

She hugged me. I felt like my mother's arms had just wrapped around me. "I know something that might help you. Have you ever tried meditation? I've had my issues too and this helped me."

After our loving embrace, she held my shoulders with both of her hands and looked deeply into my eyes. "I know you'll find the peace you need. Let me give you something. I know in my heart this will help you."

She quickly rummaged through her purse.

"Here it is." She placed the booklet into my hand and placed hers on top of it. "This is a guide that will explain everything. I suggest you start tonight, and skip going to bars after work from now on."

That night I read the meditation guide, followed the instructions, and said a prayer asking for healing and God's mercy on my soul. I sat quietly on my bed in the lotus position and attempted to clear my mind of all thought as instructed by the guide. It was difficult at first, but each time my thoughts tried to take over, I was able to steer my mind back to that nothingness described in my meditation booklet. After what seemed like a couple of hours into this meditation, I thought I saw a gentle pulsing light with what the book described as my "mind's eye" and it broke my peaceful concentration. I opened my eyes to find a bright, laser-pointer-like white light twinkling on my wall near the edge of the ceiling.

I wrinkled my brow and crossed my arms. "I thought I was having *an experience.*" Even so this light seemed different. It was centered within a dark oval shadow that appeared to be a black hole on my wall.

I stood up to investigate and moved the drapes from my window to alter the beam. It didn't. *The light must be coming from a reflection off my watch.* But the beam could not be broken, not even when I waved my hand in front of it. "Now that's just weird," I said out loud. *The light is coming from the wall.*

I moved back to the corner of my bed and stared at the twinkling light. It seemed to be changing shapes with hints of color while it slowly became larger and brighter. The dark area also slowly increased in size as the light intensified. I was mesmerized. At one point, the light unfolded like a butterfly emerging from a cocoon. I saw a tiny winged shape. It reminded me of a paper cutout of an angel. I smiled. *Now this is getting interesting. The book didn't mention this part.*

Time seemed to slow down when the shape suddenly became crystal clear. I rubbed my eyes, and dropped my hands to my side. *Oh my God!*

Before me was a perfectly defined angelic entity within the black window-like portal on my wall. When I first saw it clearly it was about the size of a Barbie doll, but it continued to get larger as it drew closer to my room. I lost all sense of time.

When the angel reached the edge of my room, the black oval enlarged to the size of my entire wall. My thoughts raced as the angelic entity emerged from the portal. She had the most Divine face I'd ever seen, beyond all the paintings and books I'd come across in my life—a pure, classic beauty. She was larger than a human—approximately six-and a half to seven feet tall, adorned in a thin, white *robe, a simple braided rope around her waist*, a delicate tiara seated on her head, and plain sandals wrapped her feet—exactly what you'd expect, but more. I could feel only pure love radiating through my body within her presence. The whole figure was ghost-like, shimmering white, and semi-transparent—almost as if she was made of light. She exuded a nobleness that made me feel like I was in the presence of royalty. Her wings were shaped like those of a dove and her hair gracefully curled around her celestial face.

I was awed by the size and beauty of her wings. The perfectly formed wings stretched out nearly four feet from each of her shoulders. I focused on the details of every feather intimately as she slowly floated forward. I was nose-to-nose with her, and I leaned back as I became slightly cross-eyed to keep focused on her beautiful face. She then greeted me with a momentary kiss before backing up. I felt a love in my heart like no other I'd ever experienced in my life when she touched me. Taking in the whole vision, she instantly reminded me of a quintessential Greek or Roman statue. She was a goddess.

Here I was, simple me, face-to-face with one of God's supreme messengers. I felt loving warmth throughout my body. When I closed my eyes, I could see a celestial light with my minds-eye that was emitting from her upon me. I felt healing.

At that moment, I fuzzily realized that I could have asked any of the questions we seem to always ask about God and creation.

What's the purpose of life?

What happens when we die?

Do we have past lives?

What's a soul?

Does hell exist?

Instead of asking a question of profound import, I straightened my back, shrugged my shoulders and raised my hands out in front of me, almost in disbelief. "So, what are we doing here?" Not exactly my brightest moment.

So simple. So human.

Although she didn't speak, somehow I had the sense that she could read my mind. I tested this theory by thinking of a really corny joke. "What did the boy bear say to the girl bear on Valentine's Day? I love you beary much!" *Ugh...another one of my stellar moments.*

She half-smiled just like the Mona Lisa, which, in turn, made me smile and snicker.

So you can read my mind. She blinked and nodded in affirmation.

While I marveled at the thought that I just made an angel smile, the light of the universe began radiating from her. My entire body, every fiber of my being, was suddenly at complete peace—beyond love, beyond happiness—just peace. It was as if I was being hit with a gentle pulsing light made from pure unconditional love. My soul was healed. *This is what heaven is. This is what God is.*

The heavenly light continued to pour into my body, and she slowly lifted her hand with the index finger extended. While watching this movement unfold, I was suddenly reminded of the outstretched "hand of God" painted on the ceiling of the Sistine Chapel by Michelangelo. She reached out and gently touched my forehead between my eyes, opening my mind to the all of the love in the universe.

I gently closed my eyes and lost all sense of time. My body grew warmer as thousands of spiritual messages began flowing into me. The messages came to me in the form of pictures from a rapid slideshow and thoughts from elsewhere that permeated my mind. It was as if my thoughts and another's were merged into one.

I wasn't on my planned life path. I was supposed to be helping people, especially youth, to teach them the importance of kindness and compassion. I had a purpose to fulfill and I needed to move away from the detrimental and destructive course I was on.

It's all up to me.

I have a choice.

I always had a choice.

Never have fear again.

I am healed.

I surveyed the life I had created for myself in this moment of moments and I was way off the course I was placed here on Earth to follow. I knew I was engulfed in negativity, but now I could see how to transcend it and help others do the same.

While Divine messages swirled around in my head, the angel gradually floated away from me into the enlarged portal. Her figure slowly diminished as the distance between us grew, but she never stopped smiling at me. Her light became a single focused point, and then it was gone.

I sat in astonishment for a few minutes, shook my head and ran to the bathroom to look at myself in the mirror. For some reason, I needed to see my own face. *You know what just happened, don't you? You know now! You know God exists! Why you?*

Why me? I frowned and pointed my thumb into my chest.

My reflection shook a finger back at me. "You can't tell anyone about this, they'll think you're crazy," I said out loud. "You'll be put into a straight jacket! No! You have to keep this to yourself. You'll just have to live with the gift of knowing. Your life is changed...forever."

I felt as if my soul had been rebooted, like a computer with a fresh new operating system. I had new knowledge but much of it was archived for now to all be revealed at the right time in my life. My entire life plan was laid out before me.

I know it's all true. There is a God...angels do exist...her name is Gabriel. She told me! But how? There were no words, but I have them in my mind. People really have been seeing these beings for centuries...everyone needs to know! They all need to know it will be okay. But who's going to believe me?

I continued to interrogate my reflection and asked a question I already knew the answer to: *So, what are you going to do with this?* I knew that all of the answers were given to me and others would unfold consciously when I was ready for them.

It was all in my hands now. My life. My love. It all had new meaning.

I felt so alone, yet paradoxically, I felt connected to everyone and everything at the same time. I no longer feared death and I was somehow completely renewed with the precious gift of loving and wanting to live my life.

Suddenly I was back with my father in his room as I heard him move in his chair. I sat quietly, still immersed in that experience all over again, reflecting on how my life had radically changed since that encounter.

I raised my hand to my chin and darted my eyes to the floor. "I've tried to do my best. I have, Pop. You know that. You've seen the volunteer work I do. I've tried to be a bit kinder to others, but I'm not perfect. No one is. We're all flawed and that's the beauty of life. Right, Pop?"

My dad's stoic face didn't change. The room felt completely empty. I could only hope he understood everything I said.

I paused for another minute in silence, and then got up to ask a staff member to bring my father something to eat. Before I departed, I sat next to him and said, "We'll all be together again on the other side and Mom will be waiting for us. I know it."

He nodded slightly, perhaps in agreement. I hugged him, and stood up. "Goodnight, Pop. I love you."

Later that night, my mother passed away. It was Mother's Day. *How beautiful!*

My sister, brother and I, along with our three spouses, gathered at my father's room in the early morning to break the news to him.

My sister surveyed each of us. "Who's gonna tell him?"

My brother slumped against the wall next to my father's door. "I'll do it. I thought of the words last night just after Mom passed away," he said.

My brother looked down at his shoes, drew in a deep breath and entered my father's room. "Pop. Mom's gone."

"Yeah, I figured it was her time. When can I see her?"

We were all fumbling in the hallway to listen in on my father's reaction to the news. We quickly composed ourselves and slipped into his room in solidarity.

"We'll take you now, Dad. We're all here for you. We're a family and we're all one with this," my sister said. "We all want to see her together."

I knew no one wanted to go through a display of uncontrollable grief. The night before my brother had pulled me aside and said, "How are we going to deal with this and keep Pop from giving up when we lose Mom?"

Our emotions were on a hair trigger and we didn't have the reserves to deal with an extreme level of sorrow, especially from our patriarch.

The entire time we were together, I was in silent agony wondering if my father believed what I had shared him the night before. But, I wasn't sad in that moment. I knew my mother was in the most loving hands in our entire Universe.

"Please let that help him through this moment," I prayed silently.

We approached my mother's room with trepidation. Not one

of us knew what we would encounter and how we would react emotionally. When we entered, we found that the nursing home staff had posed her with a small smile on her face and a red rose in her hands. She was at peace.

"She looks beautiful," my father said. "No more pain. No more suffering for my sweetie. She's with God now."

His tender words lifted the veil of pain from the room like a dove soaring into the long-awaited sunrise.

"Thank God this went well," my sister whispered to my brother and me. We nodded in affirmation.

A short time later, my father was taken back to his room and I stopped in to check on him. My mother's younger brother was visiting. As I entered the room, my father immediately looked up at me smiling and said, "Bobby. Tell your Uncle Dan about the angel."

———⟶∞⟵———

I've thought about the angel every day of my life since that encounter. I've deeply pondered the gifts she gave me and the one thing she took from me—*faith*. Seems odd that I've lost faith, but faith to me is a trust in something you're not sure exists. My faith was simply replaced with unequivocal *belief*.

Believe.

DECODES

Believe

If you have a mountain of pain before you, or you're lost in a cold valley of shadowy doubt, know that God's healing hand is there to mend your broken heart and an angel's smile is always looking over your shoulder to guide you. Faith is a divine blessing. Believe and you will be blessed with a peaceful life, filled with hope and love.

Trust

I know this may sound like a cliché, but saying a prayer every day does work. Every one of your prayers is heard. You may not always get exactly what you've prayed for, but you will always receive what you need. God has a plan for everyone and that includes you. When you employ God as your architect, don't worry about the details of the plan—just know it's the right one for you. Love is always part of the design.

Share Grace

Every day of your life is filled with God's grace; and every second you have choice to share this Divine blessing with someone else. We're all links in an infinite chain of love. Never be the weakest link in this chain. Love matters. Kindness matters. Life matters.

Love Finds A Way

I was lost
I was alone
Only two feet
To take me home.

I lost many friends
I had no place
Only my thoughts,
An angel's face.

I took one step
Then another
My only guide
The Holy Father.

I had fear
And I had doubt;
I could only cry
I couldn't shout.

I gathered strength
Fell to my knees
Prayed for hope
Love set me free.

I followed the light
To a new day
For this is how
I found my way.

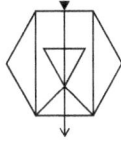

REVERSE CLIMBS

"Everything that happens to you in life, good and bad, provides lessons from which you can learn and grow spiritually. Always look for that lesson, and shine within the silver linings you discover along the way."

— Robert Clancy

Most would agree that any journey takes careful preparation. Did you pack the right items? Do you have the right equipment? Enough food and water? Try to imagine every day that you are embarking on a unique journey—a journey of the heart. The only equipment required is your smile, a small case of kindness, and your love. Travel light. When planning a trip with your soul, extra baggage is not needed.

When you're not prepared, or just careless, not all trips are pleasant. When you take an "exit" from your life path, it's easy to fall into negative thought patterns and overlook the wonderful things that make you a beautiful soul. While traveling these dark trails, fear can grip your heart, imprisoning you in your own personal hell. Fear not, and you are freed to wander in the garden of love and forgiveness. For some, it's not that easy, because they fail to simply ask for help.

When the shadows of sadness darken your heart, reach out to your family and friends. Each person can bring a small ray of hope and light into your life. Even the smallest candle can brighten a darkened room.

—◦◦◦—

As the waiter was delivering our lunch, I slid my chair back from the table and tossed my hands into the air.

"What do you mean you've never been further west than Fredonia, New York?" I teased my friend Ron. "Man. You need to get out there and see this wonderful world we live in! We have so many wonders right here our own country. Think of all the great things to see just in the Southwest - the Grand Canyon, Monument Valley, Zion National Park, and *Las Vegas, baby!*"

Little did I know that my playful antics had planted a powerful seed—one that grew quickly. It turned out to be the prelude to the greatest adventure of our friendship.

I raised my glass in jest. "To our excellent adventure to the Southwest. You get the plane tickets and I'll plan the itinerary!" *Clink!* Our two glasses came together, sealing our fate.

Although I'd traveled to the West Coast, I'd never been to *any* of the places I recommended to Ron, so I really didn't know what I was talking about. In fact, I was just joking about the Southwest travel. I soon learned that Ron did not get the joke.

A week later, I received the call. "I have the tickets!" Ron exclaimed. "We leave August 9th!"

"Tickets? Tickets for what?" I asked in confusion. "Leave August 9th? For where?"

"Phoenix!" he announced. "Phoenix, *Arizona,* of course. I thought that would be a good starting point for our Southwest odyssey. We can spend a couple of days exploring Phoenix, then we'll be off to the Grand Canyon, Las Vegas by the weekend, over to the Hoover Dam, and back to Phoenix."

"You're joking, right?" I asked in disbelief. He made it sound so simple.

"Nope. We're going. Eleven days total!"

"Okay," I said slowly, surrendering to the *fait accompli* laid before me. "I guess I'll start planning our itinerary."

"You'd better! We've got a lot of ground to cover. That reminds me, I have to book our rental car."

And that's how our adventure got underway. We planned out the things we wanted to do, and at the top of our list was hiking down to the Grand Canyon floor. Sitting 2,459 miles away at my kitchen table, I had no idea how profound this experience would be.

From a light moment at lunch to a lift-off, we went! In eleven days, Ron and I logged more than 3,000 miles on our rental car. We saw it all, too. We hiked around the rim of Meteor Crater, marveled at the Petrified Forest in The Painted Desert, played in the red sand of Monument Valley, pretended to be mountain men at Flagstaff, screamed until our heads hurt in a long tunnel at Zion National Park, and we spent half a day at Bryce Canyon in Utah. We traveled to really out-of-the-way places, such as the Old West mining town of Pioche, Nevada, and centuries-old Indian ruins hidden in the desert. There were so many red and bronze colors for my eyes to drink in, at times I felt like I was on Mars - long-gone from the *U-S-of-A*.

The Grand Canyon.

Yeah, that's where my life changed. We arrived at the gates of this revered national park late in the afternoon, just in time to grab a quick bite before heading out to watch the sunset cascade over the majestic landscape. I stepped toward the canyon edge and thought "Whoa! Where the hell is the fence around this thing?" I was accustomed to the overly-safe (and fenced-in) Thacher State Park, situated along New York's Helderberg Escarpment, just minutes from my home.

As the sun was setting, a beautiful full moon was rising to greet us. *This is just a perfect night.* Everyone around us seemed at utter peace with nature.

"This has to be one of the most incredible sights I've ever seen," the man standing next to us said.

With a smile, I replied, "This is something everyone needs to experience at least once in their life. How could I have almost missed this one on my bucket list?"

The man chuckled. Ron, wanting to contribute to the moment, broke the mood by blurting out one of his ever-present, obscure facts. "Did you know that there are around two fatalities every year at the Grand Canyon? I read about an unfortunate couple who accidentally put their car in drive rather than reverse. I think they were parked somewhere just over there," he remarked as he made a sailing motion with his hand. "Well... they plummeted to their deaths. There was nothing the park rangers could do. It took the rangers two weeks to recover the bodies."

"*Okay,*" I exclaimed while pulling my dangling feet back from the edge of the one-mile deep chasm. "I think I could have guessed what happened, but thanks for ruining my peaceful moment."

"I was just sharing the facts," Ron countered with a smirk.

"I guess that really puts things into perspective now, doesn't it?" the man next to us chimed in. "You should always know what you're getting yourself into."

Very soon, I would come to discover *exactly* what that statement meant.

As we planned for our hike to the base of the canyon the following morning, I couldn't stop thinking about the people who perished in such a beautiful place.

"I won't be clumsy and fall over the edge," I kept saying silently to myself. "I'm very careful and that won't happen to me."

Ron carefully unfolded the map. "So, which trail should we take for our hike?"

Looking over the various trails, the name "Bright Angel Trail" jumped out at me. "How bad can this one be? After all it has the word *angel* in it," I said confidently.

"Sounds good to me," he agreed. "We leave at six-thirty sharp... in the A.M., that is! We'll need to pack a couple of waters, a snack, and our lunch. We can pick up sandwiches tonight at that convenience store around the corner."

The next morning, we were so excited that we decided to walk the two miles from the hotel to the trailhead just to take in more of the Grand Canyon experience. By the time we reached the top of Bright Angel, we had encountered a few people who were finishing their hike out. They were loaded up with high-end backpacks and looked as if they'd been to hell and back, certainly nowhere heavenly. Their emotionless, ashen-colored faces featured sunken eyes that never looked up at us. They were mutely staring at their trudging feet as they plodded one foot in front of the other

"Are they *that* out of shape?" I judged as I moved past them and took my first step on the trail.

About an hour into our hike, I remarked to Ron, "This is easy. Look at the time we're making!"

I marveled as my physical stamina seemed to receive a boost with the passing of every zombie-like hiker making their way up the trail.

I drew in a deep breath and broke into a huge smile, surveying the mesmerizing floor of the canyon. "Can you believe this view? I think this is the first time in my life that I've seen people on a trail below that actually looked like marching ants. How far down is that?"

"Statistically speaking, it's a little less than a mile," Ron pointed out as he stopped and took a big swig of water.

From our vantage point, we could see the winding trail on the canyon floor that led to a small structure. The marching ants were going in and coming out at almost the same rate.

"That can't be a gift shop down there," I said pointing at the tiny building.

"I'm not sure what that is, but everyone seems to be going in and out in a hurry."

"That's where you get your water," a park ranger said as he suddenly appeared next to us, wiping sweat from his brow. "Trust me, you're gonna need it. You're walking into a desert after all. Make sure you always have some water on your person. We lose people on this trail every year."

I noticed his hat was soaked with sweat and his face was drained of color just like the others hiking out. It was the first time I noticed how hot it was. As we walked away, every step we took suddenly seemed like it was accompanied by a rise of degree in temperature.

"Thank you, sir. Point taken," I said brightly, even giving him a quick salute. But my thoughts were elsewhere.

How can someone get lost on this trail? There's only one way down, and one way out. The park rangers here must not look too hard for lost hikers.

Two hours more into the hike, we encountered a wooden sign that illuminated his comment. It was emblazoned with the word *WARNING!* in large red letters across the top. The fine print read:

If you choose to pass this sign without at least four liters of water on your person, you do so at your own risk. We will not be able to rescue you or recover your body for some time. Each year, hikers suffer serious illness or death from exhaustion.

Below the warning message a hiker had scrawled "*...and have a nice day!*" For extra emphasis, they added a smiley face next to the U.S. National Park Service logo.

It was at this very moment that Ron's morbid story, the words of the man from the night before, and the park ranger's warning began rattling around in my brain.

"*Or* recover your body?" I quipped. "What do they mean '*or recover your body*'? Shouldn't they try to save you first?"

"Have a nice day, indeed!" Ron said. "This canyon covers about 1.2 million acres and is on average ten miles wide. The maximum width is 18 miles. There aren't enough park rangers to cover this much ground. We're really on our own here."

Ron's last statistic was the only one I cared about at this moment.

"Uh... maybe we should rest for a bit, eat something, and check our supplies," I tossed out. I wanted to think about this latest development.

I knew we had less than one bottle of water left for each of us. We'd been carelessly drinking it on the way down. Technically, I knew we were ill-prepared for the hike, yet I felt fine physically. The hike up to this point had not been strenuous at all.

Weighing all this, I threw caution into the hot wind and said, "Maybe we can go a little further to check things out. After all, when will we be back here again?"

We had hiked for another hour before we decided to turn around. The marching ants on the canyon floor didn't look any bigger and the ominous words *"recover your body"* were motivating me to change course.

Hiking *down* into a canyon and then *out* is what they call a *reverse climb*. The easier part—climbing down—happens first. The strenuous work begins when you climb up and out. In general, it will take you between two and three times as long climbing out as it does going down.

At this point, we'd hiked down for about five hours. Imagine climbing a rocky, unstable staircase for hours on end—no elevator, no drinking fountains, and no place to rest. To say we were ill-prepared is putting it mildly.

How could I have been so stupid?

By the time we reached the trailhead, it was well after dusk. We could barely put one foot in front of the other, our eyes were sunken, faces ashen. And we still had an additional two-mile walk back to our hotel. We were involuntarily groaning, convinced that our thigh muscles were about to explode.

"Why didn't we bring the car here?" I grumbled.

That night, as I lay on the hotel bed, sunburned and aching all over, I thought about the people who lost their lives on the trails of the Grand Canyon. How many were unprepared and unaware of the perils, just like me? How many ignored the signs as they continued downward, just like me? How many didn't ask for help when they got into trouble?

Pondering all this, I realized that people take *reverse climbs* in life, too. They exit from their life path, thinking they're going somewhere better, or intentionally someplace worse. It's an easy road to hit rock bottom. Some people eventually do make their way back out. Others are less fortunate. They just never come back—poor choices, drugs, alcohol, and negative people are found all around these exits to nowhere. The abysmal hike down Bright Angel Trail carried an important lesson – one that I was grateful to live through and learn from.

When we checked out of our hotel the following morning, the receptionist overheard us talking about our hike. "Did you make it to the bottom? Which trail did you take?" she inquired.

"Bright Angel Trail. And *no*, we didn't make it all the way down. I'm still feeling this one," I replied while gingerly massaging my thighs.

With a knowing smile she said, "Don't feel bad. Not many people hike all the way down. After all, the nickname for that trail is *Satan's Staircase*."

—⚮—

When you exit your life path, it takes a lot of work to come back. There are no easy ways around it. The further down you go, the more help and support you will need, but it's there. *You just have to ask for it.*

Family and friends are there to help you pick up the pieces of your broken heart or your shattered dreams. There's always someone who cares about you and loves you more than you know. This is what holds the love in your heart together.

When you finally make the choice to turn around, *really* make the choice, you may ask yourself, "How many chances does God need to save my soul?"

The answer is simple—*as many as it takes.*

If you're on a road that leads nowhere, there is always time to change direction. You just have to follow love's light out of the shadows of despair. The choice is always in your hands, but it needs to be in your heart also.

Whether you're on a mountain of success, or you've hit rock bottom, the heavens are always above you. Have you taken the time to look up lately?

Just as a journey of a thousand miles starts with the first step, a journey in love never ends, but it does require that you take that first step in the right direction—no matter how small.

Decodes

It's Okay to Ask for Help
It's okay to admit you're struggling, but you must acknowledge this within yourself. It doesn't matter how rich or poor you are, or what position you hold in life. Everyone is struggling with something. If you find yourself in a reverse climb, reach for help. When you do, you will have made the first step in your journey back to the top.

Discover Your True Path
Your true path is always tied to your passion.
Complete these sentences:

My passion is _____.
I am _____.

Whatever you write for these sentences becomes your reality. Once you know your clear direction, create a vision board. Take a piece of large card stock or poster board and glue or tape on pictures and words that relate in some way to where you want to take your passion. Place this board in a location where you will see it every day. This is a powerful visual representation of your dreams, and it tells your subconscious mind that you are serious. Dreamers aren't lost in thought. They're just going places no one has ever imagined. Dream big! Attain your dreams!

Know Your True Worth

Your worth is not determined by the size of your bank account, but rather the capacity of your heart to hold love for others. Realize how special you are. Each of us has a unique talent that no one else on this planet has. Develop it! A true superhero knows who they are deep inside, and they know who they need to become for the greater good of humanity.

You are a superhero!

BALANCE

*"Balance in life isn't about making everything
equal, it's about sharing equal parts of your
heart for each area of your life."*— Robert Clancy

•

There are three essential parts to obtaining balance in one's
life—mind, body, and spirit. At any given time, one or more
of these aspects may become unbalanced. For example, when
your mind becomes stressed and overwhelmed, you need to
raise the areas of your spirit and body to compensate for the
disharmony. This can be easily achieved by doing physical
exercise and an activity to uplift your spirit.

Exercise elevates your body's immune system. There are
a host of benefits derived from physical activity described
by the medical community—from increased serotonin levels
that improve mood to increased circulation of white blood
cells that stave off illness. Simple exercise might look like a
routine of walking, jogging, push-ups, and aerobics. Even gentle
stretching for five minutes can have a positive impact.

Couple movement with an activity to enhance your spirit—
meditating, spending quality time with family and friends,
feel good activities like volunteering, or simply sharing your
beautiful smile—and you'll be able to offset your stressors.

I know what you're thinking; what if all three areas become
imbalanced? The good news is there's a fourth "dimension" that
governs the other three—*Divine Consciousness*—which rests in

a *neutral state* until we assign a *value* of positive or negative to a situation.

At any moment, we can harness this consciousness and move our bodies, minds, and spirits back into balance, but the power to do so comes from the mindset of assigning *positive values* to each stressed area. This outcome is achieved through the state of gratitude.

Think of it like this: If you're apprehensive because you're writing a large check to pay a bill, the universe may respond by continuing to give you unease about your wealth so you won't be able to write that check the next time. Why? You assigned a *negative value* to the domain of money and the universe will always give us more of what we focus on. Instead, give thanks and be grateful that you had the cash on hand to make the payment. This positive outlook allows the universe to bring more abundance to you.

Each day, your life is a blank canvas and you have a choice about how you are going to paint it. We create our reality, and it is the result of where we place our energy and attention. Are you assigning a positive or negative value to each facet of your life? If you choose to frame your experiences with a positive view and diligently look for the silver linings no matter what is occurring, *Divine Consciousness* will respond with more experiences to reinforce that upward spiral.

Just like you, I'm not immune to putting negative labels on myself or my stressors. It's easy fall into this adverse mindset. As the end of my mother's life began to unfold, I was agonizing over her health. She had stage-four cancer and began to experience dementia and memory loss. I negatively colored my perception of this time in her life by saying things like, "I'm losing her. She's not going to know me. I'll be a stranger in her life."

Once I looked within my heart, I discovered the wonderful

tenderness and joy of this situation. I consciously changed the value of the stressor of my mother's failing health to a positive one. Each of us has the capacity to reverse our negative labels.

The cancer that consumed my mother with worry and pain when she was lucid was all but forgotten by her. She lived her remaining days in a state of true happiness. My family rejoiced that the cancer never again affected her mood in a negative way, and this probably extended her life. She never forgot I was her son, and I enjoyed many meaningful interactions with her during her precious final days. I learned a great lesson about gratitude and the power of my mindset.

With loss, there also exists the opportunity for love and happiness to surround you—just like there is a chance each day that you will be engulfed in the radiant light of the sun. You wouldn't know and appreciate the *good* without experiencing the *bad*. Although you can't change some of the events in your life, you do have the choice to balance them with how you label them. Give thanks for all the blessings you have and the universe will always bring more of the same.

———∞———

The room was filled with suits and the white noise of hundreds of conversations. I saw someone I knew and moved toward the middle of the crowd to greet her. A man I did not know broke away from a conversation and turned toward me as I approached, so I stopped and extended my hand. "Hi, I'm Robert. It's great to meet you. What do you think of the conference so far?"

He shook my hand and adjusted his name tag. "Great to meet you Robert...my name is Bill. Great crowd here. Just too many conversations about all these terrorist attacks and school shootings. What's the world coming to? There's so much negativity out there these days. I'm worried the world is changing for the bad."

"I hear you, but I've always tried to focus on the good in people. I know beyond a doubt that there are more loving and compassionate people in this world than not. Isn't that why we're all here? To learn to be loving? It's not as bad as people or the news agencies frame it to be. We're just constantly bombarded with negative news."

"If we're supposed to be loving and compassionate, and this is our prime directive as you just said, then why is there is so much war, suffering, and sorrow in the world?"

Bill's question made me pause. This was an unexpected conversation for a business networking event. After another moment of reflection, I responded with a single word. *Balance.*

He cracked a smile. "You're right. You're absolutely right."

It was an enlightening moment for both of us.

Later, I reflected more deeply on the concept of *balance* in the context of my *life.*

Balance is woven into the fabric of the universe in much the same way that love is the thread that binds it together. Balance is constantly sought, yet everything is in a perpetual, sometimes chaotic, state of movement. It's this give-and-take struggle for neutrality that allows for never-ending, infinite possibilities. It's up to us to label all the resulting occurrences in a positive way to tip the scale in the favor of love and peace.

I think of life as our soul's elementary school, where we are all given an opportunity to learn the fundamentals of love. We are all children in God's eyes and life is our playground. Just like the playgrounds of childhood where we experienced laughter and exhilaration, and sometimes suffering, we learned to appreciate the positive times because of the juxtaposition of how we felt when we were in pain. We are here on this planet to learn through these *contrasts*.

How can you expect a child to understand the concept of heat without also allowing them to get burned or experience cold?

The answer to any issue always lies within the framework of *balance*, in the same way the darkest of nights is followed by a brightly lit sunrise. Choose to trust in your heart that the dawn will come again; it eventually will, because darkness can't exist without light. Without darkness, you wouldn't enjoy the sunshine. Without ugliness, you wouldn't understand beauty. Value the things that bring you joy because, without the challenges you've faced, you wouldn't fully appreciate the very things you cherish, but more importantly you wouldn't be who you are. Never let a negative experience define who you are, let it define just how much stronger you've become.

Your destiny is not so much determined by what happens to you, but by how you respond to life's lessons. You can't control everything that occurs in your life, but you can control how you view it, how you'll let it affect you and how you'll grow from it. I'm simply in awe of those who, after all they've been through, can still hold their weary heads so high. These broken souls are my true heroes.

Ask yourself, when you encounter devastating setbacks: Have you become a wiser, stronger, better and more empowered person? Do you appreciate kindness more? Do you give thanks for all the blessings still in your life?

To be fully part of the universe, the depths of your soul must appreciate and understand how much love matters, because it truly does. To choose and know love through both sides of balance is to have lived completely. You have so much to bring to the world by just being you.

Your life is a precious gift.

Your love is truly limitless.

Only you create your reality...make it a positive one!

—∞—

There's no room left on the canvas for fear and doubt when your life is balanced with faith and hope. Keep a positive outlook, trust in the bigger picture painted for you each day of your precious life, and give thanks for every silver lining you discover there.

DECODES

Take Balance Breaks

There are two kinds of *balance breaks* you can add to your daily routine. First, reflect upon how deeply love has impacted your life in positive ways. In the morning, practice a gratitude affirmation for all your blessings. This could be about the first time you understood kindness or something as recent as a simple smile you received the day before. Write each of your gratitude thoughts in a journal. Second, take a "peace break" from your negative thoughts. In the afternoon or evening, find a quiet place and slowly fill your mind with everything you're thankful for that day. If you can't think of anything, be thankful you're alive, you have breath, and that someone is breathing easier because you've lived. These mini vacations lead you to happiness, peace, and harmony within your body, mind, and spirit.

Adapt to Change

Seemingly negative events are always wrapped with something positive or beneficial, even if we can't recognize it initially. The seeds for something new are always planted in what came before. Your challenge is to take each life change in stride and adapt with positivity. Instead of dwelling on the past, keep focused on looking for the seedlings of new growth.

Release Mistakes

We're all human and we are all souls surrounded by that humanity. And yes, we make mistakes. The popular quote by Alexander Pope says it best: "To err is human," but this quote has an even more important second part that's often left off. It is: "To forgive, divine." Forgiveness has to start with ourselves. Each day, release one of the errors you've negatively labeled yourself with. Write it down, or better yet, draw a picture of what you are releasing from your life, then destroy that piece of paper, releasing it back to the Universe.

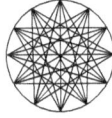

CLUTTER

LEE'S STORY

"Droplets of rain are God's way of cleansing the earth, allowing life to grow. The next time you cry in sorrow, think of your tears as God's way of cleansing your soul so you can grow spiritually."— Robert Clancy

Why do we tend to hang on to emotional baggage? Is it our human nature? What purpose does holding on to a past we cannot change, or creating a negative future, serve, other than to impede our present growth and happiness? The past and future are merely reflections of the mind. They cease to exist when we simply let go of them. The only thing you have is the *now*, and *now* is the place where you live fully.

Are negative emotions—such as sadness, anger, and frustration—tied to our past issues worth keeping in our minds and hearts? In the grand scheme of things, does being upset or holding on to something you cannot change have any positive impact on improving your current situation? Why are you feeling this way? Is it to get the attention of someone you love, or do you have a deep-seated fear?

The greatest spiritual breakthrough occurs when you are able to control the one thing you can—yourself. To do this, you must first relinquish that control to the Divine.

There's a vast difference between owning your happiness and bargaining for it. When you seek love or happiness by negotiating with a past you cannot change, it will slip through your fingers every time. Instead, focus your love on the present. Everything you'll ever need comes from what you have in your life at this very moment. What you are currently blessed with will always outweigh any emotional baggage you are carrying. *Isn't it time for you to finally let it go?*

What you manifest with your mind comes right back into your life, because the Universe has a *return to sender* stamp on every one of your thoughts. Whenever you hold negative emotions, you become a beacon for negativity to find you. Although it may be difficult to do in the heat of an issue, try to control yourself, and frame your thoughts in a more positive way. You might be pleasantly surprised at the outcome. Love never discriminates. Love doesn't judge. Love just accepts, but you also have to accept that love.

Happiness does not come from the money in your bank; it is a dividend paid on the interest you accumulate whenever you are in a state of love.

What are you banking on for your *life's saving?*

—∞—

The smell of freshly-brewed coffee permeated the air as I casually dropped into my morning routine of browsing my Facebook feed. Almost immediately, something caught my eye: "That's an odd picture to post. I hope everything is okay with her husband."

Puzzled by the picture I was seeing, I clicked on my friend Susan's profile to see what was going on in her life. She is a dynamic, successful business attorney from my professional networking group. Vibrant and full of life, both Susan and her husband are two people I admire. All the members of my networking group hold them in high regard.

I nearly spilled my coffee onto my laptop as I reread her

post. *Oh my God! He passed away! How? When?*

I read on: "*For those of you who wish to attend, my husband's wake is this afternoon. The details are below. I appreciate your thoughts and prayers during this difficult time.*"

I didn't know Susan beyond our networking group, but I instantly knew that I needed to attend this service. It was just my way—simply being present in quiet support. I shook my head in disbelief and dumped my coffee into the sink, stomach churning. *I can't believe he's gone.*

That evening, I slipped into the church for the wake, awestruck by how grand the building was. The grandeur was in stark contrast to how empty the massive space felt with very few attendees. Family members and friends were in line for the viewing, but not the number I was somehow expecting. *Where is everyone? Am I early?*

When I reached the front of the line, Susan visibly brightened and wrapped her arms around me. "Lee, I am so happy to see you. It means the world to me that you're here. Your enthusiasm and spirit is something I truly need today. I'm deeply touched that you cared enough to attend."

"I am here for you," I said without hesitation. "If you need anything, do not hesitate to reach out to me. It's the least I can do."

She smiled for a moment and placed her hand on top of mine. "You are a special person."

I left the service feeling like I made a small difference, but I wanted to do more. I just didn't know Susan well enough to know *what* to do for her.

Four months after the funeral, I saw a posting from Susan on Facebook asking for help. She was cleaning her house the following day to prepare it for sale. I immediately saw the chance to do that "something more," and replied to her post: "I need to check my calendar, but if I'm free, I'll be there. What can I bring?"

A response came quickly: "*Thank you Lee! Busy hands are happy hands. Woo-hoo! Just bring that amazing spirit, bright smile, and kick-butt work ethic! That should do it.*" It was the cheerful type of response I expected from Susan. Still, I wondered how she was *really* doing.

I smiled as I looked at the sun beaming through my kitchen window. I was excited to lend a hand—anything to reduce Susan's burden of losing her spouse. I hoped she was doing better. I couldn't imagine how devastating something like that must be. He was the other half of their *dynamic duo*. I knew I'd have some big shoes to fill tomorrow.

The next morning, I grabbed my coffee and pulled up Susan's Facebook post to see who else was coming. My heart sank. *Are you kidding me? Only one other person offered to help?*

When I arrived at Susan's home, I found the garage door open. I waded through a mountain of cardboard moving boxes and poked my head through the kitchen doorway. "I'm here to help!"

"Lee! Thank you! Thank you! Thank you!"

We weren't close friends, but when Susan hugged me, it was so tight that I felt like a family member. I also felt there was something more she needed to share with me.

I surveyed her backyard through the kitchen window, and saw two men on her deck cleaning and dismantling a Jacuzzi. "I see some other helpers have arrived. How are you doing? Or, uh, I mean holding up?"

"I'm fine," she responded quickly. "I'm just trying to get everything straightened out—organized. I'm trying to...." Her eyes suddenly welled up as her voice trailed off. "You don't know what happened, do you?"

"No, and I don't need to."

Her body slumped as she gazed at the deck and brought tightly clenched fists to her chest. "He killed himself out there."

I was stunned. I took her hands in mine, and looked deeply into her eyes, trying to bring her focus away from the deck.

She continued: "Those guys out there are volunteers from my church. They're removing the hot tub... where he did it. If I get rid of that *thing*, it will at least take away some of my anger, my betrayal, my pain."

We hugged silently for a few minutes. I took a deep breath, but found I had no words. I then realized that the greatest gift I could give Susan was to just listen.

"All that's left in the house is memories—mostly things that remind me of this awful event. I need you to help me with packing them up. I have so much to go through. So much to sort out."

Internally trying to digest what I had just heard, my practical side took over. I pointed at one of the boxes and said, "If you don't need it, why keep it? This is just stuff. If it bothers you, *get rid of it*."

She closed her eyes for a second and looked out to the sky through the window. "You're right. You are absolutely right."

After returning home that evening, I received a Facebook message from Susan: "*Lee, thank you for showing up and clearing out the house with me. That meant the world to me! More than you'll ever know. After you left, I decided that the work was done and that I didn't need to go back. It's time for me to move forward. Your love and support rocked it for me!*"

———◯✕◯———

You can be your own worst enemy when it comes to negative reinforcement. Success is often only one positive thought away. The people who've made the greatest positive impact in our world are the ones who started by making small, positive changes within themselves. Be blessed, be thankful, for today is the first day of the rest of your life.

DECODES

Live in the Now
Before you start your day, take a moment to reflect upon as many things as you can think of that you're blessed with in your life *right now*. Be present to those thoughts. What is past is just that—*past*. Time is about living in the moment so your beautiful future can unfold.

Chart a New Course
If life is stagnant, you may need to chart a new course for yourself. Choose faith to chart your life course. Allow hope to be the star that guides you on that journey, and you'll always arrive at a destination of love.

Accept Change
Change can be disruptive, but only if you allow it to be. Great renewal is always born from change. If you find that your life hasn't been a smooth sail, know the winds of change will eventually take you to a peaceful shore. There will always be setbacks, but they're never permanent. The sun will always rise again, and the weather will always clear after a storm. Remind yourself of your blessings, set your sights on a new goal, and persevere. When the goal is love—*simply love.*

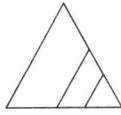

No Limits

"The only limits love has are those you've imposed upon it with your own heart."— Robert Clancy

◉

Do you know your true limits? Have you ever been fully tested? Limits only exist in your own mind. The test comes when you stop believing in everything you are capable of. When you strip away everything that lessens your precious life...all your fears, your doubts, and your worries, you will find one thing remains...faith. You'll be as strong as an oak tree when you believe in the strength of your roots; you shed what is needed for your growth, and you forever reach upward for the light.

———⌖———

As part of my weekly fitness routine, I swim laps at my local YMCA. I am not a strong swimmer, by any account. When I first started this regiment, I would moderately swim about ten laps or so, get a bit fatigued, and stop. I didn't want to over do it. This lightweight routine continued until I had an awakening while hiking a strenuous part of the Appalachian Trail in the White Mountains of New Hampshire.

I started my hike with plenty of water and snacks, so I thought. The weather predicted on the various mountains I planned to summit was twenty to thirty degrees cooler than the base camp I was at. I packed a heavy sweatshirt, a jacket, and a hoodie to accommodate the expected drop in climate. An hour into the hike, the humidity and temperature rose well above all the predications. Once I climbed above the tree line, it was ungodly hot and humid. There was no shade to speak of, and water quickly became a premium.

After summiting four peaks, I began the strenuous return trip back to the base camp hut. This required me to summit those very same peaks. Ugh! At this point, I only had a half bottle of water remaining. My legs felt like jelly, and I was facing eight more miles of arduous climbing, or a night on the mountain without the required survival supplies. Have you ever climbed a few flights of stairs and felt that burning in your thighs? Think of the pain you'd have after climbing stairs for eleven hours, and these stairs were made of uneven boulders. I renamed them God's staircases.

I was hurting, and my thoughts raced. *Boy, you are an idiot for not taking that extra bottle of water. What were you thinking! You should have rationed your water! You're in deep trouble now!*

My worries were not unfounded. Even the most experienced hikers on the trail were very low or completely out of water. Each hiker I encountered was worried about the risks of dehydration. There was no cell phone service, and no rescue party coming. The only way I was getting off that mountain was by my own two legs, and a whole lot of fortitude.

I reached the first of the three remaining peaks and took an account of my dwindling supplies. I had just enough water to wet my tongue a couple more times, half of a granola bar, and a bit of sunscreen left in my backpack. Oh, and let's not forget that heavy sweatshirt I had stuffed in there. My t-shirt was completely soaked with sweat, and even the brim of my hat dripped with it. I was beginning to feel the dizzying effects of dehydration. While I crouched next to a large rock in a failed attempt to get out of the sun, a young man flopped his backpack on the ground next to me. He pulled out a bottle filled with dirty water and took a sip.

"To get some water, my dad and I had to dig a hole in some mud we found off the trail back there. This tastes as nasty as it looks."

I held out my nearly empty bottle. "Your muddy elixir is starting to look pretty good at this point my friend."

My mind was reeling, and sweat streamed down my cheeks. *Are you going to make it back tonight? The longer you sit here, the longer it's gonna take.*

I didn't even want to stand up. I just wanted a large glass of lemonade, and would have paid anything for a small cup of it.

Suddenly, the young man's father stumbled onto the summit, feebly pointed forward, and wiped the sweat off his forehead. His breathing was labored. "One of the hiker's I passed back there told me there's a fresh water spring a quarter of a mile off the trail by the next trailhead. It's about two miles ahead of us from here."

This was just the motivation I needed to get moving again. *There's my goal! I just need to place one foot in front of the other. As long as I'm moving forward I'll be getting closer that fresh cold cup of water.*

I pulled myself up, buckled my backpack, and marched on—this time I was wearing a big smile. Up to this point, I'd been so concerned about the pain in my legs, I failed to fully appreciate the wonderful views or the incredible peace I had before me. I stopped and took a deep breath. *"You can do this! God's math is in everything around you, and it all adds up to one thing...love. Drink it in. You can do this!"*

Life truly is a series of peaks and valleys. Although some of the valleys are filled with pain, the peaks always take you one step closer to the glorious light...and that light is always within you!

When I reached the trailhead at the fresh water spring, I dropped to my knees and rejoiced. That cup of water ranked up there with one of the best tasting swigs of water I've ever had in my life. It was the extra boost I needed.

It took me several more hours of labored hiking, but I made it back to the hut with a smile on my face. I can't say it was easy, but the change in my attitude propelled me to new heights I didn't know existed within myself.

I pushed myself well beyond both my physical and mental limits, and discovered something that is beyond those physical limitations—indomitable spirit.

While I lay in my bunk bed that night, I took a moment to reflect - what else have I been holding back upon? What have I left on the table that I could have finished, made better, or reached with just a little push? I learned how to begin everything without expectations, and to love without reservations so I will always be without limitations.

When I returned to the YMCA on the week following my hike, I swam twice as many laps in half of the time I made on my best days.

———⟨⟩⟨⟩———

All the peaks and valleys of your life have heavenly views. If you always look up, you'll never miss any of them.

Decodes

Have No Expectations

Expectations limit your experiences. Have you ever had the perfect vacation, then gone back to that same place and it just didn't live up to that first time? Think of what you may have missed out on the second time around because you tried to recreate something that no longer exists. It's the past. You need to live for now, and now doesn't have an expectation.

Persevere

Perseverance is having the fortitude to overcome life's challenges, but it's also having the faith to never let go of hope and the courage to never stop believing in yourself. You can do and achieve anything you set your mind to, just don't give up.

Find Strength in Peace

All of your strength comes from the divine grace that lives within your heart, but it is also in everything that surrounds you. You can bring peace to any moment of your life when you just stop long enough to see it.

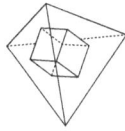

THE BLACK BOX

"Love conquers any obstacle of the heart. When your valley of doubt seems so deep, your legs will become too weary to cross it, let hope be your strength's saving grace. If your mountain of pain is so steep you can no longer scale it, let faith carry your spirit higher than any mountaintop can ever reach." — Robert Clancy

---

We all have one...there's an area of your soul I've labeled the *black box*. This dark place is where you store all those things that seem too painful to deal with in your life. The *black box* can contain your deepest fears, your doubts, regrets, the *unspoken things* you may not want others to know about you. This is quite possibly because you feel you'd be judged or rejected by those around you if they knew this about you. Do you feel there is something holding you back from moving forward in life? Do you have bouts of fear or doubt when it comes to the image of yourself and how others see you?

If you answered yes to any of these questions, you could have a *black box* laying dormant in your soul. Your *black box* could even contain something you didn't know was in there. This could be a life issue you simply repressed in order to move on, but ultimately, this blockage may be holding you back.

It important to know you are flawed—everyone is. Even flawed diamonds shine in their inherent brilliance when they seek the light. Opening your *black box* exposes it to this light, and this is how you will shine again. You will never be judged in God's eyes by telling the truth. You can only be misjudged by those who are unwilling to accept the truth you've told. Trust that in the end, it will be okay. Listen with your heart to the lessons of this journey, and believe in the truth discovered in your purpose.

So, how can you begin?

The first step is to take it slow and reflect. Releasing everything from your *black box* all at once can be overwhelming. The best place to start is with inner reflection and meditation. Find a comfortable, darkened place to sit quietly. I often light a candle and play soothing new age music in the room where I meditate. Close your eyes, and focus on your natural breathing. It's good practice to select a word or mantra that you repeat silently in your mind for a short while at the beginning of the meditation. I find that great words to use for a mantra are love, hope, peace, inner-beauty, kindness, abundance, or healing.

When I begin a meditation, I often visualize a gentle light coming down upon my head that flows down though my body, through my feet, and into the earth. As this light slowly flows through me, I relax each part of my body that I visualize it touching. Then, try to clear your mind of all thoughts and distractions. Each time your mind begins to wander, try to gently steer your thoughts back to your selected mantra.

I find the daily meditations to be beneficial in many ways. Outside of the reduction of stress, meditation brings a centering to one's life. Think about how many times you bounce out of bed and run through your day. Just taking that extra few minutes in the morning to put a smile on your face by experiencing gratitude for your own existence can set you up for a much better day. There are so many stressors facing our life—especially young people. Just think about the frequency with which we are bombarded with negative news. Learning to know your soul through inner peace helps contribute to a satisfied life.

When you've completed your meditation, listen to your soul for the message it brings you. Identifying the true nature of your *black box* item is a huge part of the healing process. This is the time to ask why this affects you so much, and identify what areas of your life it impacts.

The second step is to release. Find someone close to you whom you trust. It's important that this person is someone who you believe won't change their perception of you, or worse, pity you. This person should be a trusted, caring confidant in your life. Find a quiet space to simply talk with them. Let them know you trust them, and ask them if they are willing to help you by just listening to you without judgment. Be honest and completely open in your discussions with this person. Speak truth to release your heart gracefully. Know that this truth you speak is for your precious heart and this is forever held in that beautiful grace. Trust that you are simply releasing your burdens. Take solace in knowing that love weighs nothing, yet it weighs in on everything in your life.

Now it's time to heal through renewal. You will have an open wound exposed to the light. Just like any wound, it takes time, loving care, and attention to properly heal. This is a key time to not waste any energy worrying about tomorrow, or wondering about what you could've or should've changed in the past. This is time to spend with yourself. It's completely natural to be withdrawn from life for a while.

Light wins every battle with the darkness, just like hope overpowers all fear and doubt. This is the dance of life. Stay positive during this time! Your thoughts dictate your words and actions, and those actions are the embodiment of your soul. This is a critical time to give gratitude for everything you do have in life. Attitude truly is everything, especially when that outlook on your life comes from deep within your soul. Whatever you've released from your *black box* is gone forever. You can and will heal from this pain if you believe in the divine light within your heart.

—◯✕◯—

The sun will still rise over the ashes of a broken life. Let the winds of faith carry your ashes to a place of renewal. Allow hope to be the seed that's planted firmly on this new ground. Let love be the nourishment that helps you grow strong again.

Decodes

Reflect

What you see in the mirror is a simple reflection of what surrounds you. What you see in your heart is the reflection of everything you are and were ever meant to be. Look within to see who you truly are, and believe it.

Release

Be empowered to let go of what no longer serves you. Your heart has all the permission it will ever need to release those things from your life that bring it down.

Renew

Every renewal creates a chance for abundance. Never be afraid to grow in a new direction. Change is good. It creates these opportunities. All you have to do is seize them. They are yours.

Vision

Steve's Story

"It is not your eyes, but rather your heart that has the ability to see true beauty."— Robert Clancy

●

The beauty of love is that it sees no color, no race, no religion and no creed. Love just accepts you for who you are...a precious spirit with your flaws and all. There is nothing more beautiful in this world than your ability to paint a smile on another's lips with unconditional love....and it's easy to do! The wonder that surrounds you is a mere reflection of everything that's within your heart. When you seek inner-beauty in your life, you will find what love truly is.

What if you celebrated everyone you met as if they were the most important person in your life? Life itself would become the beautiful festival it's meant to be. Every single day would be filled with smiles and laughter, because even at your most trying times, you would know without doubt that someone else truly cares about you. Look around you. These people are already in your life. Recognize them. It takes no effort to share a kind word or a smile with them. A kind heart is where love makes its home. Isn't it time you came home?

Do you realize how beautiful you are? God created your soul from all the splendor of the universe. Know that your exquisite image is revered in heaven for all time. The angels sing your praise each and every day as God continues to shape the lovely masterpiece that is you. Know your true beauty.

———⌘———

His fingers gently draped over the top of his camera, as the light bouncing off the photography umbrellas illuminated his face. "The eyes are the windows to the soul, and the dance of the light in my lens is what captures it. It's how I see into their spirit—every precious moment of their lives."

It was the first time I fully understood what my father did for a living. He didn't *just* take pictures of people, he captured their soul in a fleeting second. I came to learn that he was one of Long Island's prominent portrait photographers, but he was always much more than that to me. He knew what true beauty was and he could snatch it out of the air with the click of a shutter. That precious revealing moment comes and goes in the blink of an eye, but my father always seemed to know that perfect timing. It was through years of working by his side that I discovered that the human face, with its infinite variety of expressions, is where one's essence resides—this discovery has fascinated me ever since. I could have never foreseen that my journey to discover what my father captured on film would lead me to a spiritual revelation—something I could only see with my heart.

I loved photography and just being with him, but he relentlessly lectured me to take a different path. "You've got your whole life ahead of you. Have you thought about where you'd like to go to college? Why don't you become a doctor like your cousin, Mel. There's someone you can look up to!"

I've always admired Mel. I loved to stay at his house—it was my refuge—the place I'd go back to time after time to reassess my life. His home always provided that escape for me, partially because Mel and his wife were such kind souls, but also because the house itself held a mystique. His house was originally designed as the Italian consulate. It was a large four-story, stucco-covered Italianesque castle-like structure, adorned with pictures, artwork, and artifacts of Mel's many world travels. I'd spend hours lost in my imagination just looking at everything.

I learned so much about life there. After nearly every dinner, we were entertained by stories of Mel's adventures—and he had many. He'd sit back with his pipe in one hand, furrow his bushy gray eyebrows to tell tale after tale of the strange lands he visited.

He was always thinking about the human condition—how he could help people, especially the impoverished; he was a true doctor. There's an old Hebrew phrase that describes his heart—*tikkun olam*, which means *repairing the world*. This perfectly describes Mel's life path.

On a whim, he once built a school in the Dominican Republic, and then went on to start health clinics in third-world countries where none existed. Though his unbound kindness, he transformed the lives of some of the most destitute of people on our planet. The most wonderful thing about him was he didn't need to help with any of these causes! He just did.

Through his eyes, I learned the true meaning of what a humanitarian is. He's the epitome of that word. He'd just go out there to make a positive difference, no mater how crazy the idea.

In my late teens I experienced how Mel handled tragedy with grace. I was on one of my many pilgrimages at his house when he received a phone call that changed his life. I could tell by his expression that the news on the other end of the line was terrible.

"He's alive? Thank God! Where did the plane go down? Oh my God...burned? How bad?"

No one in the house blinked as he carefully hung up the phone. We were stunned as he methodically doled out the terrible news about his best friend.

"It's Alan. He was in a horrific plane crash today. He's in an intensive care burn unit. Thank God he's still alive. He'll have a tough road ahead, but I'll be there for him every step of the way...we'll need to be. Friends are part of our family, and we care for them the same. "

Mel, being the consummate physician, spent the next several hours calling the hospital to gather every detail of Alan's condition. Although the prognosis wasn't good, Mel remained focused and committed to doing whatever he could to help.

During the weeks and months that followed, Mel kept in constant contact with Alan to encourage him to move forward in the wake of the challenges he now faced.

Alan's recovery was slow and painful, but a little over a year after the accident, he made an unexpected appearance at one of Mel's parties. His injuries were extensive. The flames had robbed him of his facial features and several fingers. I have to admit, I was in shock at how he now looked. I struggled to make sense of his *new face*.

Everything I learned about the subtleties of the human face came from the knowledge my father passed on to me, but these features were non-existent in Alan.

By then, I had a good handle on how to properly use a camera. I learned to take cues from the subtle configuration of soft tissue that gives each face its distinctive appearance— the mouth, lips, cheeks, and eyes activated in a precise way to tell me when to press the shutter. In Alan's case, the shutter in my mind was at a loss. We're taught in our society to either look away from, or even worse, stare at people with disfigurements—this moment haunted me for years.

Luckily Alan brought some clarity to me that evening. During one of our conversations, he said, "Burns are democratic. It can happen to anyone, at any time. Recovery is far more painful than the burns ever were, but I will make it through that. I'll do something with this...something positive."

His words not only gave me insight into his soul, but a beautiful insight into the souls of all those who've survived this kind of trauma—something that has always stayed with me.

———∞———

Several years later I was off to visit Mel again. I was excited to catch up with him, and to hear about his upcoming adventures. In his usual posture before he announced one of his quests, he glanced over the top of his horn-rimmed glasses at his captive audience, and straightened up his tweed jacket. I was brimming with anticipation.

"So, I decided I'm going to bring vision to the indigenous people located on the Atlantic coast of Nicaragua—specifically eyeglasses. I will need several assistants to help me get volunteer optometrists—we need them. Do you think you can assist with this?"

I practically leaped out of my skin. "Absolutely!"

I was always honored to be worthy of Mel's respect, but now I had a chance to really prove myself. The beauty in this endeavor was how simple and inexpensive it was. Mel recruited twenty undergrads from William's College to pool their resources to purchase *scratch and dent* reading glasses from local stores for about twenty-five cents a pair. One of Mel's friends, a professor at the New England School of Optometry, created a simple eye chart test that could easily determine an individual's correct prescription in a remote field operation.

To give me deeper understanding, Mel had me watch a video of a previous William's College humanitarian trip to Nicaragua. His intent was to give me an appreciation of what I was now a part of. He could tell by my look that I was somewhat unimpressed with the presentation.

He furrowed his brow, and the corner of his lips curled. "Okay. What wrong with it?"

"Well, not to take away form their wonderful efforts, the video itself is a bit long, not very polished, and it doesn't capture everything they're trying to say. It just doesn't tell their story very well. It's not compelling, and that's a shame considering the positive impact they made there."

"Do you think you can do better in capturing this with your lens?"

"I'd love the opportunity to try."

He extended both of his hands and cracked a huge smile. "It's settled then. You're coming with us. Our story needs to be told properly, and you're just the person to tell it."

I was beaming with excitement. I'd waited years to fulfill two life-long ambitions. One was to go on an adventure with Mel, and the other was to be a National Geographic photographer. The second dream wasn't truly being fulfilled by this trip, but it was as close as I'd ever come to it.

From the first moment my feet touched the ground in Nicaragua, I was in culture shock. The streets were covered in mud and trash. Wild, malnourished dogs roamed the streets looking for scraps of food. The buildings were in complete disrepair and neglect, and the people living there weren't much better off.

I was trained to extract beauty from my subjects. My eyes struggled to find it, at first, in this destitute place, but Mel's ever-present positive attitude pushed me to look harder. Then it happened...like a light breaking through the dawn clouds, I saw the most incredible smile on a child who had just been fitted with glasses. For the first time in his life, he was able to see clearly.

Mel patted me on the shoulder. "You see that? *That's* why were here."

My heart opened as wide as my eyes that day. I began to see true beauty in the human condition. Love, no matter how faint, is brighter than any darkness could ever be. This is what Mel *wanted* me to see. That's what I *needed* to see.

Through Mel's philanthropic effort, and the generous donations he obtained, nearly two thousand people received glasses, per week, during our stay.

—∝○—

Alan took me on the next odyssey into my soul. He, like Mel, wasn't one to sit still in the face of adversity or challenges.

Following a visit with a young boy at his local burn center, Alan realized the importance of peer support for those with burn injuries. He quickly establish one of the first burn support organizations in the United States, which then inspired him to found The Phoenix Society, a nonprofit organization dedicated to empowering anyone affected by a burn injury.

Years later, I had the honor to see the magnitude of what Alan created first-hand when Mel and I were invited to attend The Phoenix Society's annual International Burn Congress—an event that brings together hundreds of burn survivors, their families, caregivers, burn care professionals, and firefighters from around the world. By this time, The Phoenix Society had now grown to over ten thousand members strong worldwide.

I was a little reluctant to bring my camera, but Mel insisted.

I wasn't planning on doing an elaborate photo shoot, so I only packed my camera, a couple of lenses, a few rolls of film, and my essentials. I thought I might grab a few shots of the city, and maybe take a couple of picture at the event. I was in for a surprise.

When we arrived, I surveyed the lobby of the hotel and noticed many people streaming into the hotel who's faces were wrapped with scarves. Their clothes also covered nearly every inch of their skin. In their newly-found comfort, they all began to reveal themselves one-by-one by removing the garments that covered their scars. As each emerged, their postures transitioned from one of avoidance to one of confidence. In this moment, I had a fleeting thought, "I need to capture this."

A short while later, Alan and his wife, Delwyn, greeted me. As I was shaking Alan's hand, I blurted out, "Do you think any of these people would be willing to sit for a portrait?" Before I could retract my words, Alan's eyes lit up.

"What a great idea! This is brilliant. You should document their stories. After all, I just happen to have one of the best portrait photographers right here on site."

I quickly lifted my hands in protest. "Oh no! I couldn't. I don't even have all of my equipment with me. What about the lighting? Um, er...they won't want their portraits done here."

"Nonsense," Delwyn exclaimed. "I will start getting them scheduled for you right now."

Alan peered at me with conviction. "I'll make an announcement too. You'll be able to pull this off. I have faith in you. This is important!"

My mind was reeling. I could barely look most of the attendees in the eye, let alone figure out how to set up a makeshift portrait studio with the limited resources I had.

Alan's reassurance motivated me, but my heart was pounding. "You'll have two days to get this done. If anyone can do this, I know you can."

That night, I thought about how our society is obsessed with beauty standards that few of us can live up to. Why is it that deformity is misunderstood and often shunned? How could I confront this issue head-on with my heart and my camera?

The next morning, I spent a couple of hours scouting the hotel to try to find suitable areas where the lighting would be adequate for a portrait shoot. I found an ideal location near the lobby, and I set up shop.

I have to admit, I was not prepared for the challenges I faced photographing the burn survivors I encountered at the conference. In many instances, all the recognizable facial features we rely on to comprehend personality and emotion were missing, literally burned off. Because fingers are particularly vulnerable to the devastation of fire, many of these people were without fingers or hands. This led to several awkward handshakes.

Under normal circumstances, it would be uncomfortable and impolite to stare at a burn survivor, but I had been invited to do just that. The privilege was not lost on me. My camera gave me the permission to carefully observe each of them—every detail.

The sessions became, as good portraiture always does, a collaboration between myself and those who sat in front of my lens. My heart filled with each of their incredible stories of survival. Such intimacy gave me a greater understanding of the human condition and the resiliency of spirit that allows us to rise above unimaginable adversity. I gained a deep knowledge of what true beauty is through the strength possessed by each of the people. I began to see the world differently now. Beauty is truly found within each of our souls.

Following the photo shoot, I spent a great deal of time wondering if I had done my subjects justice. When I looked at the photo collection in its entirety, I knew I had something powerful and meaningful. I knew I was now entrusted with a responsibility to do something with these images, but didn't know what that was.

It was nearly a year later when I received the answer to the question that gnawed at my soul. I came across an announcement of a photo gallery opening up in my hometown and quickly made contact with the owner, Mark Kelly, to schedule a meeting for a review my portfolio.

At our initial meeting, I first displayed the cache of images from Nicaragua and Mark was impressed. "These are good. These are really good."

My heart lifted, and I laid out the portraitures of the burn survivors. "So what do you think of these?"

Mark's reaction was immediate, but not what I expected. "Do you know what you've just done?"

My mind was swimming, *"Had I just offended him?"*

I'm sure he sensed my confusion as he oddly rolled up both of his pant legs. "These are my burn scars and skin grafts. Do you have any idea how powerfully healing these images are? You've captured something incredible here. Let's get this show scheduled, and we're publishing a book of this as well."

During the photography exhibit at Mark's gallery, I was pulled aside by a burn survivor who drove several hours to attend the show.

With tears steaming down her cheeks, she wrapped her arms around me. "I have to tell you, I don't go out much...for obvious reasons, but after hearing about this exhibition and your story, I was compelled to attend. I'm so glad I did. You capture my soul in these photos. You know what true beauty is, and I now know I'm still all of that."

———∞———

More beauty is found in a simple act of kindness than you'll ever see on the cover of a fashion magazine or in some other human ideal.

When you color the world with your beautiful essence, let red be the soft rose petals of love you've placed upon another's lips. Allow blue to be the heavens that reign over your fertile valleys of hope. May yellow be the radiant sun that forever warms your heart. Choose white to become the peaceful purity you find within your soul, and let purple be the embroidered robe of faith that wraps your life with God's hands.

True vision...being able to see how beautiful you truly are!

For more information on the Phoenix Society and the Phoenix World Burn Congress, please visit phoenix-society.org

Decodes

Be an Old Soul

Old souls may be the ones who've been around the block a few times, but they're also the ones who know how vastly beautiful that block is; they're the ones who still stop to smell the roses, and they always stop to drink in every small moment of life.

Have Gratitude

Give thanks for the family the surrounds you. Give thanks for the love that surrounds you. Give thanks that God's grace has found you. Just give thanks with all your heart!

Shine

The precious light behind your beautiful eyes was meant to light this world! Share a smile with a random people today. Collect each one that is returned with your heart.

SELF-WORTH

"Don't let someone's lack of investment in your heart determine your worth. You are a priceless, beautiful soul."— Robert Clancy

●

Just by being who you are, you create positive ripples in the universe and those waves are endless. Never underestimate the light you bring to the world with your beautiful smile, your loving heart, and your radiant enthusiasm in this life. Your true beauty resides in the sparkle deep within your eyes. Become the warrior you are meant to be. That's right—a warrior! Never let a negative experience define who you are, let it define just how much stronger you've become because of it. Of all the challenges you've faced, you can only be made better for them. Just as all the great masterworks of art have weathered the wrath of time, only to become more revered in their inherent beauty, you too are counted among them.

There are many factors that have shaped your personality. For example, environmental influences—such as how you were raised within your family structure—may determine how you react to affection. Genetics may play a role in not only how you look, but how your mind is structured to cope with stress, doubt, fear, and negative environmental influences. The one factor that is often overlooked by most is their spirit—the grace within you. Your eternal essence can help you overcome all of life's difficulties. Rely on this inner-strength to help you rise far above any negativity stemming from your upbringing or your perceived physical limitations. I've personally witnessed and have been incredibly inspired by people who have not only transcended their personal tragedies and setbacks, but have turned these negatives into their success.

While volunteering at a suicide prevention walk, I came upon a quilt made from pictures of all the people who took their lives over the past few years. What struck me the most was how beautiful and happy they all looked. The question, "why?" kept ringing through my mind. I couldn't even begin to imagine the terrible internal struggles and pain they must have been going through. As their grief-filled families silently walked past me, I felt the incredible void left in their lives.

How critical are you of how you look? Do you hate most pictures of yourself? All the beauty and wonder you truly are comes from the reflections of your heart, rather than those in the mirror. How you see yourself is not how everyone else views you. Yep...you are your own worst critic. It's time to give your precious soul all the permission it needs to be a radiant light that dances among the shadows of all your fears and doubts.

There's a light at the end of every dark tunnel, but you're also a shining light within the darkness that someone else is following to find their way home. It's time to see all the beauty you are, and how much you're worth to everyone you've touched with your beautiful life. Be that light! You are a treasured soul...now and forever.

—∞—

You can never be devalued when you are filled with love—you simply become priceless. Love is the golden bridge between your beautiful soul and everything else. *Know your worth!*

DECODES

Be Worthy

Stop assuming what others might be thinking about you. Negative opinions are just meaningless thoughts that can add no credence to your life, unless you allow them to. When you remove the power others have over your psyche, then you become powerful.

Lose Your Critic

If you have a negative sound bite about yourself playing over and over in your head, then it's time to change the channel. Spend time with those who appreciate and support you, and most importantly, believe them when they compliment you. It's your right to whole-heartedly accept these positive affirmations.

Rise Above

We've all been cut and bruised walking through the gardens of life. When you rise above the thorns, you'll find all the sweet roses reaching toward the light. I can't say that taking the high road is easy—it's not. What it does offer you is the power to see your life from a higher perspective—one you control.

Spare Change

"It's not the fullness of your wallet, but rather the size of your generosity that matters."— Robert Clancy

●

Believing in the universal connection that binds all of humanity together in love is not a way of life, but rather a pathway for your life. Success is not the dollars you've spent or the money you've saved. It's the time you've spent saving others.

Adding at least one act of kindness to your daily routine will not only change the lives of those around you, it will also change you in infinitely positive ways. This can be as simple as letting the person behind you in the checkout line go ahead of you, skipping the first spot you find open at the gas station, or just passing on a smile.

Sharing is one of the first acts of compassion we learn as a child. When we are young, it is difficult for us to learn to share because we don't fully understand the power of this precious gesture. It often takes consistent encouragement from others to learn this behavior—a true gift we give to each other. Think of the first time you can recall sharing something that was meaningful for you—gingerly handing over a favorite doll or toy, giving someone else a turn on a swing just when you really got it going, letting them be the team captain instead of you. Think of the last time you saw a child share in a truly unselfish way. Did it warm your heart? Giving always has love attached as its "return to sender."

Your "why me?" question might be revealed to you when you cross over to the Divine. Your "what is the meaning of my life?" question is a work in progress. Never leave that question unanswered, and always try to answer it by doing something good for someone else.

You are not a human with a soul, but rather a soul surrounded by other souls under the cloak of humanity. You're only here to learn about one thing...love.

———∞———

"Can you be at our studio this Monday at twelve fifteen?" the television show host asked, handing me her business card. "We had a last minute cancellation and I would love to have you be on the show. I know it's short notice, but..."

Before she could finish, I replied, "Absolutely!" I didn't even check to see if my schedule was clear. When you have a chance to be on television talking about something you're passionate about, you just say *yes* and make it work later.

"Great! I'm so happy we met. I'm excited to interview you about volunteerism," she said. "This is a topic close to my heart. I can't wait to sit down with you."

The city district where the television studio is located is bustling at the time of day I was scheduled to arrive, so I got there early to secure a convenient parking spot. After several passes around the block, I found a less-than-ideal parking space. This one came with a Mount Everest-sized snow bank I had to scale to reach the quarter-swallowing parking meter deeply embedded in it. This put me in a less-than-perfect mood.

As I started inserting quarters into the meter, a seemingly distraught elderly woman standing at the edge of the street in her brown overcoat caught my eye. I tried to smile at her, but it ended up being more of a smirk as snow began melting into my shoes.

"This is fun," I called out sarcastically, more to the Universe than to her. More seriously, I called over to her, "Is something wrong? You look a bit stressed, too."

Her arms dropped limply to her sides and she said in a defensive voice, "I just want you to know I'm not crazy and I'm not homeless or anything like that. I'm just really embarrassed because I didn't bring enough money with me for my bus fair. I'm stranded and I can't get home. I don't want to ask anyone for help because I don't want them to think I'm destitute."

"Well, I think we've all had something like that happen to us," I replied. "I only have credit cards on me and I need these quarters for this dang parking meter, but I always have emergency spare change in my car. Hold on a minute."

I waded back through the massive snow bank to get the car and the money. As I popped open the change holder on my dashboard and grabbed enough cash for a bus fare, she called to me, "I'm really embarrassed about this. My family is going to think I can't take care of myself."

Again, I shrugged off her disclaimer and said, "Really, it's okay...I'm mean, you'll be okay."

Her disposition didn't improve. When I tried to give the money to her, she was so uneasy that she didn't lift her hand up to take it. I immediately thought, "What if this woman was my grandmother? How would I want someone to care for her?"

I carefully took her hand in mine, looked into her eyes and said, "Really, this is all right. I'm more than happy to help."

Her eyes raised a bit, but her face exhibited a hint of sadness.

I placed my other hand on her shoulder and said, "Is it all right if I ask something of you?"

With a puzzled look, she inquired, "What would that be?"

Grinning, I said, "If I give you this money, will you make someone smile today? If so, can you let that person be you?"

As the words left my mouth, a smile began to appear on her face and she said, "Thank you. You're a saint."

When I reached the television studio, I approached the show's producer and asked in all seriousness, "Did you have a hidden camera following me here? You know... testing to see if I *really* have compassion for others?"

"Huh?" he replied in puzzlement shrugging his shoulders.

I then realized that only God was filming this event.

—⊗◯—

When your heart is a camera filled with love, the pictures you store there will bring you endless joy.

It really doesn't take much to brighten someone's day. Make a commitment to yourself to be a bit better and a bit kinder. Life is too precious to be wasted and love given freely is never wasted.

Whatever you give always comes back to you ten-fold. Your thoughts and actions are like seeds planted in your soul. If you hate, you will reap hatred and sorrow. If you are kind, kindness will blossom. Love others unconditionally and the garden within your heart will always have a healthy bounty.

Your soul, when fueled by compassion and kindness, illuminates the hearts of all those around you.

Practice random acts of kindness...it can start with just your smile!

Be radiant.

DECODES

Connect

The greatest bridge you can cross in life is the one that connects your heart with someone else's. Giving of yourself is the ultimate gift of receiving.

Know Your Inner Angel

Love weighs nothing, yet it can weigh in on everything. It literally costs nothing to be kind. Every act of kindness is created with love...and a little bit of angel dust.
Be angelic today!

Be Open to Opportunity

An open heart lets all the light in, but also releases it to the world. Every moment of your life is an opportunity to share the wonders of love.

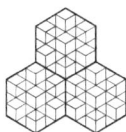

THE GIFT

"A gift of the heart need only be wrapped with a hug and bundled with joy."— Robert Clancy

⁕

You can't *run on empty*, yet there are people who wake up every day with sorrow in their hearts. It takes no effort to share a simple smile or a word or two of kindness. These gestures may seem meaningless or insignificant, but they're worth the world to anyone holding a deep emptiness. Quite often, the greatest gifts we can offer to those in need are a little compassion and simple kindness.

A flower may never get a chance to express gratitude to the sun, just like you may never be thanked for an act of kindness you performed. Take solace knowing that your light created some beauty in our world for another person.

When you choose faith to chart your life's course, and you allow hope to be the star that guides you on that journey, you'll always arrive at a destination of love and tranquility. God gave you the gift of one heart for this incredible journey, and one heart is all you'll need—as long as you share the infinite love contained within it.

———∞———

My brother bent over and gently placed his hand on our mother's hands. "Her breathing is getting much shallower. I'm not sure how much time she has, but it's not long."

The small television screen flickering the eleven o'clock news provided just enough light for me to see my brother's grave expression. The recently bustling halls of the nursing home were now completely still. The only sound in the room was the small oxygen unit supporting my mother in her final hours.

I slowly sat forward in the chair adjacent to her bed, and placed my hands against my chin. "It's only one hour until Mother's Day. That must be what she's holding out for."

"Yah. I kinda figured that, too. How's the slideshow for her funeral coming along?"

"I've got more than half of it done. I still have a ton of pictures to wade through, but I'll have it ready if it takes me all night. My laptop is set up in the lounge. I just need a break from working on it—it was getting too emotional for me. The only thing holding me together is seeing all of us in happier times."

"Yah, I hear ya. It's gotta be tough."

We took up seats on each side of my mother's bed to keep vigil. First the cancer, and now the lack of sustenance were robbing her of any remaining strength. It had been a full twenty-four hours since we had observed basic muscle movement. She had stipulated in her living will that when the inevitable time came, she did not wish to be kept alive by feeding tubes. At this point, it had been nearly fourteen days since she'd had any substantial nourishment. We sat quietly while the news faded into *Saturday Night Live*. Audience laughter was emanating from the television, but our hearts were crying.

It was just about midnight when I slowly stood up. "I better get back to working on her slideshow."

"It's all good," he responded.

I gently knelt down beside my mother's bed, and slowly brushed the hair on her forehead as I took her hand in mine. I said a simple prayer asking the angels to watch over her soul. My brother sat motionless on the other side of the bed.

I glanced over the top of my glasses and stood up. "Come and get me immediately if there are any changes in her condition. We're in this together."

"Without a doubt."

I stepped out into the community room adjacent to her room where my laptop was awaiting me, and I continued to work on organizing family photos for her funeral slideshow. I peacefully reflected on the beautiful life my mother had provided for us. She was smiling in nearly every picture I had of her—something I hadn't noticed before tonight. It was close to one A.M. when I decided to go back to her room. Even though I knew my brother would get me if she started to decline, I just wanted to be back at her side. As I walked down the hallway, I thought of everyone else in the world who's had to keep vigil for a loved one. It's all part of life—something we all have to deal with one time or another. *None of us gets out of this unscathed.*

As I entered her room, the air felt different somehow. I was by the foot of her bed when my brother's voice pierced the stillness.

"What the hell is she doing?"

My heart racing, I spun around to look my mother. I was surprised to see both of her arms completely raised up with her palms facing the ceiling. Her eyes widened as she mouthed words. She appeared to be trying to say something to someone who we couldn't see.

I eased into a smile and drew two virtual angelic wings around me with my index fingers. "I don't think you should be saying *hell*—in fact, quite the opposite. I think *they* are here for her—and you know *who* I mean."

"I've never seen anything like this...it's a miracle. She hasn't moved for two days. There's no way she could do that. She couldn't even lift her finger to scratch her chin days ago. This is just not physically possible."

"Well, it is now!"

As quickly as her arms rose up, they suddenly dropped as if they had weights attached to them. My brother was shaking his head and glancing up at me with a small smile. We carefully placed each of her now lifeless hands across her chest, and then dropped back into our respective chairs.

I'd been sitting for a few minutes when I suddenly became overwhelmed with the feeling of peace-filled divine message.

"Dave, I gotta go home. You need to call me when she passes. It's going to be in the next hour or two. This is *your* moment with her. This is *yours*."

"Are you sure?"

"I'm sure beyond all doubt."

We shook hands, pulled each other in for a hug, and I headed out to the parking lot. It was about an hour and a half later when my phone rang.

"She's gone, but just before she went, her hands lifted up one more time like they did earlier. I held her hands as she passed and my face was right next to hers. It was beautiful."

"She's at peace now and I *know* she's in good hands...God's. Try to get some sleep. I'll meet you first thing in the morning. I love you. You're a great brother."

As the daylight broke on the horizon, I arrived at the nursing home. My brother was in the lobby waiting for me. He smiled as a tear ran down his cheek.

"That was the most beautiful gift you've ever given me."

Nothing is sweeter than divine love's kiss upon your heart. Nothing is softer than an angel's wings wrapped around your beautiful soul. Nothing is more valuable than the kindness you bestow upon others.

When you trust God to be the editor of your life, and you allow His angels to tell your story, it will always end beautifully.

Decodes

Know Peace

You don't need to seek peace for it to enter your life. Peace is always right there beside you. Be still in your soul, and peace will gently walk hand-in-hand with your heart. While you're laying in bed, close your eyes, say a prayer, and think of everything you're graced with in your life. Finding inner peace is staying connected with your spiritual essence, while avoiding the distractions caused by the struggles of everyday life.

Know Your Spirit

Everything that happens to you in life, good and bad, provides lessons from which you can learn and grow spiritually. Always look for that message, and shine within the silver linings you discover there.

Trust in Truth

Wisdom is mainly comprised of two things: knowledge and intuition, but wisdom only has true worth when it is shared in faith, love, and compassion for others.

Treasured Soul

Glorious is your soul, filled with riches untold;
But none of this wealth can be bought or sold.
The diamonds you hold are all
within your heart;
Precious are your gifts; divinely created art.
All this beauty resides behind
your beautiful eyes.
Endless love to fill the heavenly skies.
Your treasure is one that's meant to be shared;
Give it freely with complete loving care.

BIG HEART
MARK'S STORY

"Paying it forward is an expense we all can afford to live with, and one that humanity can't afford to live without."— Robert Clancy

You never know exactly how much time you have on Earth, so why you should you worry about when you will die? You *should* only concern yourself with how much you share your love between this day and your last. Every act of kindness you do truly matters. Kindness is a huge piece of your soul's essence, and it's truly meant to be shared with everyone you encounter.

Just as there are infinite points within any line, there are also infinite chances for you to share your beauty each day. Being kind to those you meet on your chosen path instantly connects you with their thread of love, and thus, all of the love in the universe.

It only takes one seed to grow a mighty oak tree in the world, and in much the same way, it only takes one kind heart to grow immense love. Think about all of the seeds of love you've already planted just by sharing a smile. Have you taken a moment to enjoy this incredible garden you've created with your heart?

Compassion is the gift of empathy—the ability to form a kindred bond with another's experience. As you journey through life, marvel at all the souls that come and go from your life. You become a precious expression of each of the bonds.

Be mindful of every moment. Take time each day to make a list of all the wonderful things you should be thankful for—your family, your friends and your comforts. The number one thing at the top of this list is your own life and more importantly, your beautiful soul.

All hearts come in one size...large, but they're not always fulfilled. Make sure your heart is always filled with compassion through unconditional giving. When your heart overflows with love, you'll be surprised to find it may accidentally spill over onto others.

At the start of each day, ask yourself, "How can I be a bit kinder today?" "How can I incorporate more compassion into my daily routine?" "How can I help someone today—even if it's only in some small way?"

Simply said, kindness travels a long way—*all the way to heaven.*

———❈———

I was taking one of my many annual trips from Long Island back to upstate New York when I spotted a rusted-out, maroon Oldsmobile sedan parked on the shoulder of the highway. On the roof sat an unusually-shaped black box. Although this car caught my eye, it was something else that caught my heart. I had to stop.

"Why are you slowing down?" my wife quizzed as her eyes filled with concern. "You're *not* stopping for *that* car, are you?" she continued as her finger intently pointed at the four-wheeled rust bucket straddling the side of the road. This gave me pause for a moment, but I continued to slow our vehicle.

Glancing at our two young boys in the backseat, I shared my wife's reservation, but my lips spoke otherwise.

"Honey, I'm not sure why, but I have to stop for this car."

A bit of horror crept across my wife's face as I pulled over a short distance in front of the stranded vehicle. As I popped my door handle, my wife cautioned, "Be careful. We don't know these people, and..."

I shrugged my shoulders and smirked. "Honey, I was a wrestler in high school. I think I can handle myself. Besides, how dangerous could they be?"

Still, I was slightly nervous. It had been years since I'd stopped to help a stranded driver. Once I became a father, my focus shifted to protecting my children. Helping troubled motorists just fell off my radar...until today.

I did a quick ten-point safety check in my mind and scurried to the back of my vehicle. After grabbing a few road flares from my emergency kit, I started toward the other vehicle. Thinking the worst, I slowly approached the car like a state trooper ready to draw a weapon at the slightest indication of danger. "Are you folks okay?" I yelled, then cleared my throat. "Do you need help?"

The passenger window slowly sank into the door and a timid voice peeped out, "I think we have a flat and my husband is disabled. We've been stuck here for over an hour. We really need help. "

Peering into the vehicle, I didn't find the dangerous highway bandits I was somehow expecting. Instead, I discovered an elderly couple not unlike my own grandparents.

"Don't worry," I blurted out with a sigh of relief. "It looks like you have a flat tire on the rear driver's side. You sit right there and I will take care of this for you. Can you open your trunk so I can get to your spare tire and jack?"

"You are such a kind person for doing this," the elderly woman said with a slight tremble to her voice. "We just didn't know what we were going to do. We were so worried because it's going to be dark soon. We thought we'd be here all night," she added.

"Not a problem," I said as I headed to their trunk. "I'll see what I can do to get you back up and running."

As I hoisted the spare tire and jack out of their trunk, I thought, "I hope someone stops someday for my family when they're in need."

Glancing at my car, I noticed that my wife was now completely turned around in her seat watching the scene unfold. Attempting to calm her nerves, I waved and mouthed the words, "It's okay."

As I placed the jack under the rear of their car, I heard the squeak of metal and the low hum of a motor emanate from their vehicle.

"Hold on there a minute!" the man's voice bellowed from the driver's window.

When I glanced up, I saw the black box on the roof of the couple's car open. A platform holding a wheelchair emerged like a shimmering pearl rolling out of an oyster shell. The gears churned away slowly, rotating the wheelchair down next to the driver's side door. A few seconds later, an elderly man seated in the wheelchair appeared next to me.

"So that's what you've been hiding in that box on your roof," I chuckled. "I've never seen something like that before."

"Yep!" he exclaimed. "I want to help you...if I can," he continued. "Sometimes, I just don't feel useful."

"Sure," I quickly replied. "I'll never turn down an extra hand! Can you keep track of these lugs while I get this tire off?"

"I'd be glad to," he responded, matching my smile.

"That's quite a contraption you have there on your car," I said pointing to the unusual mechanism.

"Gives me a little more of my independence back," he responded. "This car's been a lifesaver for us...until today. She's starting to get a lot of miles on her chassis. I'm just hoping she holds out a bit longer for us."

"Once I get your spare on, she'll be ready for some more miles of pavement," I jested as I removed the lug nuts.

As I handed him the parts, I noticed his spirit seemed to be radiating with kindness. It was almost as if I could see his entire gleaming soul with my heart. To this day, I can still visualize his beaming face in my mind.

"Well, that should do it," I announced while I lowered their car back down.

I dusted my hands off, looked down at the spare tire and I immediately saw another issue. "This one's too low on air to drive with! Well, I guess it's on to *Plan B*," I announced, as I started pondering options.

"I have compressed air in my car's emergency items. It might be enough to get you to the next exit," I said, trying to reassure the man. "You should get yourself situated back into your car. It's safer in there for you."

After the man packed his wheelchair and was buckled into his seat, I jogged back to my car to explain the situation to my wife.

"Honey, I'm gonna try to help get their car to a service station so they can get their tire repaired. They've got a flat, but I think I can get enough air in it for them to limp along for a few miles. I just gotta find my can of compressed air..." my voice trailed off as I rummaged through the trunk for my can of Fix-a-Flat. "Great! Got it!" I yelled in triumph. "Now we're in business!" I ran back to the elderly couple's car like a giddy mechanic.

"This air will only hold for a few miles," I explained to them. "I'll need to follow you to the next exit to make sure you get to a mechanic. They'll be able to take care of you much better than I can do here. I know this area well and there's a gas station with a garage just off the Kingston exit."

Their eyes both filled with tears of relief. "Can we please pay you something for this?" the woman asked, giving her purse a tug.

"Are you kidding me?" I said, waving *no* with my hands. "I can't take your money. This is just something I wanted to do. How about you just pay it forward for me? You know, help someone else someday."

"I wish everyone's heart was as big as yours," she said touching her chest. "The world would be a better place."

I patted their car hood and said, "That should do it! I'll follow you to the mechanic garage. The exit is just a few miles up and you will take a right turn at the end of the ramp. The service station is just up the road from there."

They both displayed huge smiles as they nodded their heads in acknowledgment. I felt great that I had created this happiness and relief for them. We were now all on our way to the service station.

As my car trailed behind their car, I thought, "How many others passed these people without even giving them a second thought? What if I didn't stop for them?"

Suddenly, my wife's voice shook me from my thoughts. "You're such a good person for helping those people," she said. "That's why I married you."

I just smiled as I followed the couple to the station. I pulled into the lot next to them and motioned that I would speak to the mechanic on their behalf. I wanted to ensure they were in good hands before getting on my way.

"Yep. We've got everything here to fix the tire. It will be an easy patch job," the mechanic stated with confidence. "Just a small puncture. They'll be back on the road in no time flat." He hesitated, then smiled. "Uh...no pun intended."

We chuckled while I waved to the couple and gave them the *okay* sign. I happily jumped back into my vehicle and was on my way home.

Midway through the drive home, I realized that I never learned the couple's names. Not that it mattered, but in my haste to help, I never introduced myself either. I was just happy that I'd stopped to help them. That kind of joy can't be bought.

About a month after my trip, I received a large, heart-shaped card in the mail. It was strange to me because Valentine's Day was months earlier.

Inside the card I found a simple handwritten message:

Dear Mark,

We're the couple you helped on the New York State Thruway with the flat tire. Since we didn't know your name, we tracked you down by your license plate number. We hope you don't mind.

If you remember, you wouldn't take money from us for your kindness, so we made a $500 donation in your name to the American Heart Association. This is in honor of your "Big Heart."

Just "paying it forward" the best we can!

With love,
Edna & Henry

The amazing thing about love is...it can squeeze into your heart and cover the entire universe all at the same time. In the same manner that God's hands are capable of holding everyone in the world, your heart is capable of loving them all. All hearts really are *that big!*

Decodes

Be Blessed

When you wake each day, take a moment to visualize the precious treasures you have in your life. Just lie there in your bed and give thanks for all the gifts you have to share with others and they are boundless.

Share a Smile

Kindness always happens at the beginning of every smile. It takes no effort at all to pass this wonderful gift on to another. Wear it proudly.

Slow Down

Being mindful within the moments of life doesn't take your complete focus; it takes an all-embracing understanding and awareness of love. Every second you're given to witness love—on any scale—is a gift beyond measure. Look for those small instants throughout your day.

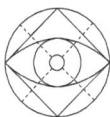

HONESTY

*"True humility is the honesty found deep
within your heart."*— Robert Clancy

Truth may exist in our spoken and written words, but only we can place it there. How often do we choose to bypass basic honesty in our daily lives? Do you skip telling the truth because you're trying to spare someone's feelings or mask something you've convinced yourself is trivial? I can only state this by admitting that I am far from perfect in this regard. Truth be told, I've failed to be honest on many occasions.

When I've had the courage to be open and truthful, I've learned that speaking honestly with someone, even at the expense of possibly hurting them, often results in a stronger, more authentic bond between us. Honesty leads to trust, and trust always leads to unconditional love.

The truth cannot survive without trust, and the furthest you can ever be from truth is when you've lost all faith.

Do you *believe* in God just because you're going along with what you've been told to think? Or do you truly *trust* that there's a divine presence in your life? When something unpleasant happens to you, if you can *trust* that you will be okay in the end, you will always be shown the truth.

Truth is ultimately the only law in the Universe.

"This guy's a menace! He's going to single-handedly bring our entire organization down. Somebody should fire him," a committee member murmured as her eyes quickly darted to the floor. Her crossed arms and pursed lips spoke volumes.

"What can we do? How am I supposed to *fire* a volunteer?" the staffing director shot back. "I don't even like being in the same room with him. I just avoid him, thank you very much!"

Normally, I don't pay attention to this kind of conversation, but the tension was too thick to ignore. It was awkward for me because I was a new board member and I didn't have a clue who they were talking about.

"Shouldn't they be a bit more discrete? I hope they don't talk like this about everyone behind their backs."

The board chair patted his hand on the table anxiously. "Okay everyone, we'll deal with this later. Maybe he won't sign up to be a volunteer again this year. At least that's my hope." A bead of sweat drip from his brow and he nervously attempted to wipe it away with the back of his hand.

"What did I get myself into?"

At the board meeting the following month, the same troublesome volunteer was brought up again—without resolution. As the months passed by, I sat through meeting after meeting listening to complaints about this volunteer named Joe and his unsavory antics. The situation just kept festering.

I was raging with questions in my mind, but never spoke it to the group: "Why doesn't someone just speak to him? Is it the avoidance of confrontation? Don't they care about the wellbeing of our organization? All they do is complain and do nothing!"

Month after month, I sat silently, my own anger festering at the lack of leadership. I could see a train wreck coming a mile away. We could lose our charter with the national organization if we continued to allow this person to compromise the safety of others. Why couldn't my fellow board members see this?

Eventually, I tried something different to get out of my own funk about *the Joe situation*. I visualized myself in Joe's shoes: How would I feel if everyone was talking about me behind my back—thinking I was a terrible person? I would appreciate the truth at the very least. Based upon the discussions I was privy to, it was clear that no one had ever taken any corrective action with Joe. I found out that he had been a volunteer for the organization for over three years. Always the same complaints levied against him—unsavory humor, safety concerns, and inappropriate behavior.

Our organization's biggest weekend leadership conference was approaching fast and I hoped that *someone* would finally speak to Joe when his name appeared again on the volunteers list. I was beginning to feel sorry for this guy. As I feared, Joe was approved as a volunteer and no one spoke with him—board members only continued to gossip and complain about him.

During the event, I kept an eye on Joe and occasionally offered corrective behavioral hints to him, but I never told him about the *whole* situation. My coaching seemed to work—or so I thought. On Sunday, I overheard two volunteers discussing a prank that Joe had played the night before on a few of the teenage staff members.

Joe had "pennied" the young staff members while they were in their rooms. This fraternity-style prank effectively turns coins jammed into a doorframe into wedges, placing enough pressure on the door that it becomes very difficult (or impossible) to open from the inside. "Pennying" locks someone in their own room against their will. While most likely done in jest, Joe's prank compromised the safety of the staff members.

To my dismay, *no one* even spoke to Joe about this incident. This was the perfect opportunity for someone on the leadership team to address their concerns with Joe, but he left the event without a care in the world. Once again, no one had stepped up.

The following year, I was elected to board chair. At the very first meeting I led, discussion about Joe's behavior flared up again.

I pushed my chair away from the table and threw my arms into the air. "I sat here all last year and you did nothing to address this issue. All you had to do was speak to him."

One of the directors dropped their chin and looked over the top of their glasses with a furrowed brow. "Well, if you think it's that easy, then I guess you can do it."

I felt my face quickly bloom into crimson. Trying to keep a smile plastered on my face I said, "Okay, I guess I will. Thanks for dropping this in *my* lap."

Because no one before me was willing to do it, I now had to face the issue, and it wasn't going to be easy. I also enjoyed the comforts of non-confrontation. I was told that Joe might attend that night's meeting.

Are you kidding me? Secretly, I hoped he wouldn't show up so I could just deal with him later in the year. Just then he walked through the door

The rest of the meeting was a blur. I couldn't focus on anything except the nasty business I was to deal with. Shortly after the meeting, I mustered the courage to speak to Joe and I pulled him aside in the hallway.

My heart was racing, I was gasping for air, and I found the same beads of sweat rolling off my forehead as my predecessor. "Joe, I don't know how to say this, but as the new board chair, I um....well, at the last year's leadership weekend I heard that you played a joke on a few of the younger staff members. Did you lock them in their rooms against their will?"

Wearing a devilish smile, he said, "Oh, the prank. Yeah, I may have uh...have had *something* to do with that. No big deal... right?"

"I know you were joking around, but this could have created a very serious and dangerous situation if there was an emergency What if there was a fire? Did you think about that?"

He stared at the floor and kicked at the carpet. "Oh come on. It was harmless. You know I didn't mean to hurt anyone. I guess it was stupid. It's not the smartest thing I've ever done."

I was determined to see this through and I locked eyes with him when his gaze came back up. "I know that's the case, but I have to tell you that the board has been pretty upset with you for a long time. Unfortunately, I've been witness to and part of the group talking about you behind your back. I'm sorry for that. But, the real issue is you've done many things that could not only cost our organization its charter, but could have had serious consequences. I'm going to have to ask you not to come back as a volunteer."

His face flushed and his cheeks went limp, but shortly after, a small smile cracked across his lips. To my surprise, he nodded in agreement. "I completely understand. I do. In light of what you've shared with me, I would fire myself. I will step away from volunteering in the future. You won't have any more issues with me."

He paused for a minute and extended his hand: "You know, you're one of the few people I've ever met who've been completely honest with me. It's a rare trait. I hope you never lose it."

———⚭———

Day cannot exist with without night and darkness cannot exist without light. But, light only contains shadows of the darkness, and darkness ceases to exist the moment light is shined on it. Truth is that light.

When you speak honestly, Divine truth and heavenly love will flow from your lips. You may speak the truth or you may speak *from* truth. The difference? Speaking the truth sometimes results in the loss of earthly love, while speaking *from the truth* in your heart encompasses a love for humanity that cannot be lost.

The truth may hurt for a little while, but lies can leave permanent scars on the hearts of everyone you've touched with them. There's only one truth written for you in the Universe. Fear is never part of that text, so don't ever edit it into your life.

Lastly, be yourself. After all, who else can be you? Strive to be true to yourself, but don't keep that truth between you and God; share this beauty with the rest of the world by unleashing all the love in your heart.

Decodes

Be Truthful

The best place where the truth is first served is within your own heart. As hard as it is to deal with, you can never be judged by telling truth. You may only be misjudged by those who are unwilling to accept the truth you've told. Know your light within and trust it, for that is where the truth is revealed to your precious soul.

Lose the Gossip

It's human nature to partake in gossip. We all love to hear the salacious stories and idly talking about someone's downfall. When I catch myself getting caught up in this type of talk, I try to place myself in the shoes of the person being talked about. How would you feel is that person was you?

Be Humble

You may have a million words of wisdom, but love is the only one that is ever needed. You are not above anyone else on this planet. When you're blinded by pride you'll fail to see true worthiness is being humble. Let your heart speak and the right words will always follow.

Faith Simplified:

Belief + Trust = Truth

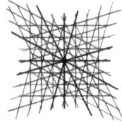

DREAMS

"Dream Bigger! Each day is another chance for you to start living the life you never imagined!"— Robert Clancy

●

In a recent interview, a host was very impressed about my accomplishment of obtaining a high rank in martial arts. He began the interview by asking me, "What kind of person does it take to make it to fifth degree black belt?" Cracking a big smile, I simply said, "A white belt who never quit."

How many times are you your own worst enemy when it comes to attaining your dreams? Quite often the only thing preventing you from your biggest goal is, frankly, you. All dreams have a chance when there is still hope in your heart. The instant you lose hope, you've lost everything. When you bring your light, your enthusiasm, and a positive attitude, you will brighten the darkest of days.

I've always viewed life as a series of peaks and valleys. Although many of the peaks and valleys are filled with difficulty, challenges, disappointment, setbacks, and sorrow, the peaks always take you one step closer to the glorious light. Long ago, I made a choice to keep climbing. I knew if I just placed one foot in front of the other, and picked myself up when I was down, I would always get to where I needed to be. Once you make it to one of those peaks, you can see the other mountain you need to conquer. Be clear in your vision. Always carry the sight of a child when you look at life. In other words, view the world with untainted love, and keep it as wild as possible! This is where dreams are made.

I believe God gives each of us just enough faith and strength to walk on an infinite path of peace, hope and love. The courage to take this journey is up to each of us by taking one hope-filled step at a time. We are not born better. We become better through the challenges we face in life.

Enthusiasm is a great catalyst for remarkable changes in one's life path. Like streetlights that guide you along a highway, positive energy will direct you to new heights you may have never dreamed of.

A few years ago, I was volunteering as a mentor at a youth leadership development seminar. There I met a remarkable young man who suffered from a rare disease that greatly limited his physical abilities. He was tethered to an oxygen tank most of the time and often required a wheelchair, but that never stopped him from participating in the volunteer projects or even the more physical activities. He just kept a smile on his face and pressed forward with everything he could do.

From the moment I met this incredible individual, I was struck by his ever-present positive attitude and his unyielding conviction to help to others. Instead of me being his mentor for the weekend, he became one of my life's great mentors through his incredible fortitude.

He taught me this beautiful lesson: Life will always provide you with challenges, but you should never see barriers. Barriers are just temporary obstructions that get tunneled through, driven around, climbed over, or simply blown up.

———∞———

Happiness is always in your hands. You cannot climb a mountain by always running away from it. The first step to conquering your fears is to face them. The views are always spectacular at all the summits of life.

Never lose your dreams or get lost in them—just make life your dream and enjoy the ride!

Decodes

Have a Can Do Attitude

A brand new day costs you nothing but a smile and a positive outlook. This day is yours...own it! When you start with an unstoppable positive attitude, everything becomes possible. In fact, nothing is impossible when you dream of the possibilities.

Accept Your Challenges

Your life may be a series of peaks and valleys, but when viewed from God's vantage point, you're simply walking upon a beautiful landscape. Take pause to see what you're facing, then push forward and conquer it. You will get there!

Seek Mentors

A black belt master martial artist can learn just as much from a white belt as they can from a grandmaster. Mentors come in all shapes and sizes. Never underestimate what you can learn from those around you. When you allow others to rise to meet their challenges, they will take you to new heights you never dreamed of.

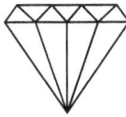

BLESSINGS

"Blessings don't grow on trees; they blossom in your heart every time you give thanks for all the beauty in your life."—Robert Clancy

●

Why sweat over the small matters in your life? Is it really worth it to expend any anguish over a tiny stain on your favorite dress or suit? Does that ding on your new car really matter? Instead, you should be dancing and rejoicing for all the blessings you have. In the sea of life, keeping your attitude in a positive latitude results in a smoother sailing day. Spread your wings, and sail on!

You have so many blessing in your life, that you can't count them all. When you fully acknowledge them with all your heart, your life will be on the road to perfect harmony. You can work hard to count your dollars, you can count your blessings that you have work, but only your true blessings count upon you. Be blessed.

———∞———

I was in a slight panic as I pulled back the curtain of my hotel window to look for nearby shops. Whenever I travel to a new place, I always pick up something to remind me of the wonderful times I've had there. Usually, this item is a small, artistic trinket from a unique shop, or a Christmas tree ornament highlighting. This time, it was different. I needed something special to commemorate a milestone in my marriage.

"Our fifteenth wedding anniversary is coming up, and I just don't know what to get her. Maybe I can pick up something while we're in town here."

"Diamonds are always a girl's best friend," Gina winked. "You can never go wrong with jewelry. I'll do some research to find the best jewelry stores in the Dallas area. We've got some time to kill before our next client meeting."

"Fifteen years...wow!" Neil exclaimed as he shook my hand. "Congratulations! Hey Gina...while you're at it, find out where the best steak house is, too. We're celebrating tonight!"

"Okay," I relented. "Just so you both know...I'm just looking. If I find something I think she'll wear, I'll get it. Otherwise, it's *Plan B*."

"Don't worry, I'll help you find something that will speak to her heart," Gina retorted with a smile.

"...and I suppose it will also speak to my wallet, but not a message I want my wallet to hear."

I had doubts about purchasing diamonds. My wife is modest when it comes to jewelry. Before we were engaged, she said, "Don't buy me an engagement ring. It's such a waste. Love isn't about diamonds. Love is about love. I don't need some glitz on my finger to remind me of that."

Her words have been in my heart ever since.

Later that day, my staff and I arrived at a respected Dallas jewelry store. It was beautifully decorated, and owned by a husband and wife. My wife and I also started a business together, so this gave me some immediate comfort.

"So, what are you looking for today?"

"Diamonds! He's looking for diamonds," Gina blurted out.

"You're a lucky guy to have a *lady* who *knows* what she wants."

My cheeks grew rosy. "Uh, no. We're not together...Um, yes, diamonds. It's my fifteenth wedding anniversary, and I'm looking for something simple, yet elegant. My wife is not the flashy type. She doesn't like rings or necklaces. Can you show me your selection of earrings?"

"Sure, they're right over here."

As I drifted around the store, I spotted the perfect pair. Simple and graceful in design—perfectly suited for my wife's taste. They were as beautiful as the sparkle in her eyes. I had to have them for her.

"Please wrap these up," I announced with confidence.

"Wow!" Gina exclaimed. "I'm so impressed. Those are absolutely stunning!"

Neil patted me on the back. "Nice one, buddy! I always knew you were the sentimental type."

It was the largest jewelry purchase I'd ever made. I couldn't wait to give them to my wife.

I was smiling ear-to-ear when I arrived home. I knew I'd hit a home run. I barely dropped my bags when I said, "Close your eyes and put out your hand. I have something very special for you."

I placed the box in her hands, and covered it with mine. "I want you to know how special you are to me. It's time for you to shine! Happy Anniversary, honey!"

As my wife opened the box, her eyes glimmered as much as the sparkling beauty in her hands.

She slowly wrapped her arms around my neck and whispered in my ear, "Oh, honey. These are wonderful. I don't think I'll ever take them off. I love you."

True to her words, these earings became a staple fixture.

She even slept with them on. The look on her face that day is something I will never forget.

It was several years later, while volunteering at a bowl-a-thon benefit for a regional non-profit, that I noticed another look on my wife's face that only a husband knows.

"What's wrong?"

In a low, solemn tone, she glanced at the floor while her hand reached for her ear, "I just noticed one of my earrings is missing, and I don't know when it fell out."

I immediately began scanning the floor. "Do you think you lost it here in the bowling alley?"

"I'm not sure. Oh, Bob, they were so expensive, weren't they?" she sighed, as she again touched the spot where the glittering orb used to be.

The shimmer from her other ear caught my eye, and I suddenly realized she was missing one of the diamond earrings. I quickly took her hands into mine.

"Yes, they were expensive, but honey, you need to put things into perspective. I know you're sad, but don't be. Just look at how many years you've enjoyed these...maybe we can make a necklace out of the remaining one. Think about the families out there who just lost *everything* they own in that devastating hurricane. If we don't find your earring, hopefully someone else does who's in a time of need. We might lose our possessions along the way, but our love is forever. Let's just have fun tonight. We're doing something good for our community. Let's just have gratitude for that."

As her shoulders relaxed, her frown changed into a smile.

"You're right," she conceded. "Thanks for reminding me of what's really important. That's why I love you so much. We are blessed."

———⊗◯———

Within all the ups and downs of life, there are always the green pastures to find in the valleys and you should always enjoy the views of heaven from those peaks. Don't sweat the small stuff. The peace you seek in your life exists in the worry you release from your heart.

Decodes

Think Big Picture

Think back to what you were worried about last year, or even a few months ago. Most likely, it's probably water under the bridge by now. How stressed were you at the time? Think about the worry and wasted energy you put into that situation. When you draw on hope, the picture of faith becomes clear.

Know What Really Matters

A new car, jewelry, and designer clothes are nice to have, but they can only bring you temporary happiness. I call it the, "buying high." Happiness cannot be bought or sold; it's a gift that grows in your heart through the love you've shared with others.

Be Unconditional

Whatever you give in life always comes back to you tenfold. Your thoughts and actions are like seeds planted in your soul. If you hate, you will reap hatred and sorrow. If you are kind, kindness will blossom. Love others unconditionally, and the garden within your heart will always have a healthy bounty.

HOPE

SCOTT'S STORY

"Hope will never leave your side, unless you choose to let go of it."— Robert Clancy

⬤

Hope is the easiest thing to lose during the most trying times of your life, yet it's the one thing you need most to carry you through them. Hopelessness doesn't come from a loss of hope—it's from a lack of faith. Casting hope to the wayside is the same as turning your back on your basic belief and your trust in the God and His great plan for you.

Why waste energy worrying about tomorrow, or about what you could've, or should've, changed in the past? Divine love exists in the *right now*. Focus on that love to heal your yesterdays and you'll lose tomorrow's doubts and fears. Everything is possible when hope is alive within your soul.

The strongest hearts are forged by fiery trials. When you allow those flames to rise, you'll brighten the hearts of everyone around you. Hope requires that imaginative spark. Your imagination can create a world of possibilities—all of which should include your healing and recovery.

A complete loss of hope leaves you feeling alone, forgotten, and abandoned—when you are not; you are always held. There is *always* someone who cares deeply about you, even if you can't see this. If you can't feel that human connection, know that an angel is always watching over your beautiful soul. God's hand is always on your shoulder, and you have an endless ocean of love around you at all times.

In times of upheaval, let love become the voice from your heart that speaks volumes without ever using words. Reflect deeply within yourself to find that inner peace. You just need a single point of light to realize you can escape the darkness. Know that this grace-filled beacon of hope eternally shines down upon each and every one of us. It only takes one ray of hope to find your way out of any void.

—⊂×⊃—

The chirps from the gurney wheels rang out as they guided me into my recovery room. Although a sterile, unpleasant scent followed me, it didn't stop a faint smile from spreading across my face. My fiancé and parents were waiting for me. "I made it! Not too bad right? How did I do?"

Their responses were elusive to my interrogation on the surgery results. *Something didn't feel right.*

The doctor entered the room, glanced over the top of my chart at me, then flipped to the next page as he delivered the news.

"We successfully removed inflamed tissue around your lymph nodes, but in the process we discovered a widespread issue throughout your abdomen. We also removed growth from your lower intestine, and the tests on it came back malignant."

My eyes widened as my heart sank. I've never been so *in the moment* in my entire life. "You mean cancer? Oh man!" My thoughts raced, seemingly faster and faster. "Will I still be able to have kids? Time to get married? How long do I have to live?"

"Slow down. You're a healthy twenty-nine-year-old man. We have effective treatments for this type of cancer," the doctor said. "You have what's called systemic Non-Hodgkins Lymphoma. I know it's a lot to absorb in this moment, but your recovery prognosis is in the highest range."

I shook my head a few times, struggling to process everything. "Systemic Non-Hodge what? How did I go from a routine check-up for stomach pain to cancer? I thought this was going to be a simple procedure?" I tried to sit up to get a better look at my family. "Did you already know about this? You knew, didn't you?"

I wasn't angry. I guess I just wanted to hear that kind of news from my family. *I just didn't want to hear it at all.*

My father gripped my leg and gave me a slight tug. "Yeah. We all knew. The doctor pulled us aside while you were in post-op. We'll all get through this together. You're strong. I know you are."

I had no idea how long or how hard this journey would actually be. I'm not the type to give up without a good fight. I immediately started a strenuous regiment of chemotherapy followed by several weeks of radiation treatment. The collateral damage from radiation was the loss of thirty-five percent of my kidney volume. I'd end up spending what felt like hundreds of hours in chemo chairs and treatments, but I achieved remission.

Marriage, kids, a life...it's all possible now!

Almost six years later, my next battle began. The cancer recurred in my abdomen. I readied myself for the fight, and began four months of harsher chemotherapy. In an attempt to take the most aggressive approach to killing the cancer cells for good, I was given a stem cell transplant. I achieved remission—I was a two-time champion. My spirits were high, my marriage was strong, and I had two beautiful children. What more could I ask for?

I was cancer-free for several more years before another tumor made its ugly reappearance. This time was different - my adversary had transformed into brain cancer. I was diagnosed with Primary Central Nervous System Lymphoma, and a new battlefield opened up. In the short-term, I had chemotherapy treatments at my regional hospital, but that would only achieve a temporary remission.

When the cancer reappeared shortly after my third remission, I was lost—*literally*. The new growth severely affected my short-term memory, causing me to lose all sense of place and time. I don't recall a single second between the end of June and mid-September of that year. I was bed-ridden and barely conscious most of the time. I was living (if you can call it that) in a constant fog for months. The last thing I clearly remember was getting an iPhone as a gift from my wife months earlier. The next thing I recalled was that summer was over and my wife was packing my suitcase.

"Where am I going?"

"Sloan Kettering. You spent ten days down there a couple of weeks ago. You're going back for your next cycle of treatments."

I sat up in my bed and lifted my palms to the air in disbelief. "How did I... or how did you...get me in there? Wait. I was at Sloan Kettering?"

As soon as I had been diagnosed with the new tumor, I researched everything there was to know about my adversary. I was determined to beat it, yet again. Over and over, Sloan Kettering in New York City came up as the best treatment center for my cancer, but the odds of getting admitted were slim. How my wife got me admitted is nothing short of a miracle—one I desperately needed.

"Honey. You did all that research months ago and I kept on it for you. You were like a broken record back then telling me over and over that it's the place you needed to be. And it is... they've done wonders for you."

"I don't know how to thank you."

She stopped folding a shirt, and looked pointedly at me. "Don't you think seeing your wonderful smile is enough for me?"

Even though my previous treatment was still a blur, hope rushed into my mind. I knew I was improving.

When we arrived at the nurse's station, I couldn't wait to get my treatments going. With most of my memory restored, I was renewed. "Just a few more treatment cycles to get through and I'm home-free!"

My wife looked over her shoulder and cracked a small smile as we entered my room. I was barely settled when a wheelchair came to an abrupt halt in front of my doorway. The man occupying the chair hissed at a nurse and slammed his fist onto the armrest. "You're a stupid wench. Gimme somethin' to eat now! You people are real jerks! You know that?"

"Sir, your room is here," the nurse said. "I'm sorry you feel that way. The kitchen is closed at the moment, but I'll try to get you some food as soon as I can."

The man then switched his focus into my room, narrowed his eyes and vigorously shook his finger at me. "Who the hell is this a-hole? I asked for a private room. I didn't request any bastards to be in here with me. This place is lousy."

My wife's jaw dropped and her brow furrowed as she scuttled past the man to the opposite side of the hall. She pulled the nurse into a hushed conversation. "How can anyone get well in this place with someone like that around? This is unacceptable. I can't leave my husband in there with an awful person like that."

"We know. We're already working on moving your husband to the room next door. We're waiting for it to open up. Please be patient." The nurse glanced back at me with a half-smile. "We thought your husband's wonderful attitude might turn him around."

My wife scoured her mind for a positive thought. "Maybe they place patients together so they'll be able to help each other. Unfortunately, this guy looks like he's been a sour pickle since he arrived. I'm not sure he can handle two battle fronts."

My wife's shoulders relaxed and tension drained from her hands. "I know you're doing your best. All of you are truly wonderful here. I couldn't bear to see my husband stuck in that room for the next week with someone like that. He's come way too far for that."

"I hate to say this, but *our friend* is now on his third roommate. I hope we can avoid rooming him with anyone else for the rest of his stay, but if you can be patient, I'll see if I can get your husband moved."

By nine o'clock that night, I was whisked off to my new room. I was alone, and the hospital bustle was settling down. Finally, I might be able get some rest.

I shook my head and rolled over in bed, reflecting on my day. *I can't believe that guy. I thought we're here to be treated for cancer, not to become it.* I was still a bit miffed, but a short time later I dozed off.

At three a.m., a crowd of hospital staff crashed into my room with a new patient, and the place lit up with a flurry of activity. Bam! There goes my peaceful night's rest.

Without anything else to do, my curiosity got the best of me, and I eavesdropped on the activity. Considering all the dreadfully sick people I'd met during the hundreds of hours I'd spent in hospitals, I felt as if I was now lying next to the sickest man I'd ever encountered. He was screaming in agony every time the medical team attempted to move him—a scream of intense pain that left marks on my soul. I was shaken and heartbroken for him. I had experienced great discomfort during my previous treatments, but I was never in that much pain.

"I think he's got severe vertigo, the worst I've seen," breathed a nurse as she closed the curtain between us. "Let's lift and roll him on the count of three. One... two... th—"

A gut-wrenching scream pierced the entire ward. I pinched my eyes closed in an instinctive attempt to blot out the sound, as tears streamed down my cheeks onto my pillow. "Please God, help this poor man."

The shrieks eventually turned into continuous moans as the staff's voices trailed off into the hallway. I strained my ears for any information on his condition. "It's gotta be the location of his tumor. We'll need to schedule another CAT scan tomorrow morning. Sam, can you get a request in for that?"

Early the next morning, the man's family arrived, with a team of doctors and nurses in tow. The privacy curtain separating us didn't offer any. I wasn't trying to listen in, but you really don't have a choice when the only thing separating you from your roommate is a thin piece of plastic in such a tiny space.

"I'm his daughter, Jennifer," one woman said. "Do you think this has something to do with a malignancy in his lymphocytes?" She continued to relay medical data to the medical team. I was amazed at the knowledge she had of brain tumors. I remember thinking that she must be a nurse, or she must have read the same medical journals I'd read.

An older woman's voice rang out next. "Hi, I'm Gloria, his mother. I just don't want my Jack to suffer. I pray to God you can get him diagnosed and get treatments going. He's a good person who doesn't deserve to suffer like he is. Please help him."

The medical team discussed possible scenarios, but I could tell they just weren't sure of his diagnosis. A swell of compassion from my heart went out to all of them. I wanted him to get the miracle treatments I received.

Over the next several days, I developed a friendship with Jack's family. I discovered that they were also victims of my previous roommate. Chuckling, I said, "Yeah, I guess he's the *other cancer* that brought us together."

"Well, at least we have one thing to be thankful for with that man," Jack's mother quipped. We all burst out laughing.

With my IV pole in tow, I spent my days walking "around the block," as I liked to call it. Fourteen laps equaled one mile. That mile was my minimum goal. Every step I took toward that mile was a step of hope. Several times, I even walked nearly three miles. On my rounds, I met many other patients and their families, but a special place developed in my heart for Jack and his family. Even though Jack was unconscious and bedridden the entire time, I learned so much about him from his family that it was as if I'd always known him.

"Jack was in a smaller hospital in our town and they got him admitted here to search for an answer. We're just so desperate. I need a miracle," his mother said.

"Did you know I was in here just five weeks ago in as bad a state as Jack? My wife worked her magic, got me admitted, and rushed me down here. I don't remember even a second of being here, but they fixed me. Give them time. Prayer does work!"

Her face lit up and she grabbed both of my hands. "You were?"

"At night, I lie in bed wondering if I'll be able to handle numbers for my engineering career, or if I'll remember sons' birthdays. But then, I think, I may lose some memories, but I won't ever lose hope. It's the one thing that cancer never took from me. I just believe that I'll survive this."

Tears were steaming down her cheeks. "You give me hope for my son."

At that very moment, my entire life changed. I felt peace encircle my soul. I'd spent so much time fighting my own cancer that I hadn't realized I was a beacon of hope for others. My life was completely renewed in this moment, but this was far beyond any remission relief or joy I'd ever experienced.

The next morning, I went home for a week off in-between treatments. I continued my "walks around the block," but these were now three-mile loops around my neighborhood. Along my path was a cemetery at the top of a large hill, hosting a large stone cross at its center. The view of the city was amazing from the base of this cross. If I made it to the top of that hill, I would be rewarded with a great view, and a rest at the foot of that cross. I would close my eyes and press my hands together.

Please God, help Jack. Help him wake up. Help him walk again. His family needs him. Please help him heal, and take his pain away.

During my week at home, I had regular chemo treatments scheduled at my local medical center. The therapy was directly injected into my brain through a port that had been surgically implanted into my head. I also took a colorful assortment of pills. Although I was in pain at times, I always reminded myself that it was less pain than some of my fellow patients were experiencing. I never lost sight of how blessed I was to have a week to be back home with my family—it was a wonderful feeling.

When I returned to Sloan Kettering, Jack had no signs of improvement. I continued to pray for him. I wasn't going to give up.

After a few days, I received incredible news that my cancer was again going into remission. I would be discharged in a few hours, once the required paperwork was completed.

I'm here for one last walk around this place, so I'd I better make the best of it. This time, I was free of the IV pole. I patted my knee, sprang up, and headed out the door from my room. "Let's get this done."

When I reached the doorway, a wobbly man holding a walker caught my eye. Two staff members in white lab coats steadied him as he passed by me. '

"Jack!" Tears welled in my eyes.

I couldn't believe it. I had prayed for this moment. I was so elated that I ran down the hallway to share in the excitement with his family, but they weren't there. I fumbled momentarily with my phone to text Jack's daughter. "He's up...your dad is walking! He's walking!"

I had barely hit the *send* button when my phone started ringing. Jack's daughter was sobbing with joy. "He's conscious? Walking? My daddy is getting better?"

"I'm looking at him right now, and he's on his feet. He has a walker and needs help with his coordination, but he's on his feet! You've got your dad back!"

I followed the aids into Jack's room, where they slowly lowered him on to the edge of his bed.

I was beaming from ear-to-ear. "Welcome back, my *friend!*"

Even though his face held confusion at my statement, it held something else...*hope.* It was like nothing I'd ever seen in my life. I stood there in awe, and imagined what it must feel like to be conscious for the first time in weeks—to *know* you're still alive, with your life ahead of you!

I then realized that's me.

If you feel your well of vibrancy has run dry, just imagine letting drops of love rain down upon your valleys of sorrow from the mountaintops of hope. Yesterday should be a distant memory; tomorrow should not be a worry. Live for *now*. Every step you take forward is on a path of love. Stay strong. Hope is always at your side.

Decodes

Stay Imaginative
If you can't image yourself getting better, healing, or in a better situation, how can you ever get there? Hope creates all possibilities in the Universe, but it's up to you to be open to them. If you think you can...you can!

Persevere
There's a solution to every problem. In some cases, you just need to persevere to find it. Your strength and courage will inspire those around you and, in turn, you will be further strengthened in your resolve. Faith gives you the courage to walk through the valley in the shadow of death. Hope gives you the strength to endure life's trials. Love gives you compassion to help others through their journeys. Don't ever give up;
hope is always an option.

Stay Positive
Your attitude directly affects your health, well-being, and everyone around you. When negativity attempts to overtake your mind, think of two positive things to counter every negative emotion. The resurgence of hope is just one positive thought away.

Hope Simplified:
Belief - Worry = Life

GRIEF

"All journeys of the heart contain valleys of despair and mountains of hope. Just know that the heavens are always above those valleys and the mountaintops touch them. To reach the summit, you just have to take one hope-filled step past all of your fear, worry and doubt."— Robert Clancy

During your lifetime, you will all lose someone dear to you. How do you deal with this loss, the overwhelming grief it brings to your life and those around you? I've thought deeply about the effect is has on one's psyche and the impact it can have on your well-being.

We each grieve in our own way and on different levels. Grief over the death of someone who was close to us, especially a child, a parent, or a close friend can cause immeasurable sorrow. This heartache can be so intense that it permeates every fiber of your being—a crippling pain that can even keep you from functioning on a basic level. There is no way to ever get over this, and you're not expected to, but there are ways to live with it—on your terms.

Whenever most people inform me that their loved one has passed, I consciously try to never say the phrase, "sorry for your loss." I know in my heart their loved one is not lost; quite often it's the person who's lost in their grief. I simply say, "Your loved one is not lost. They are found. Know they are wrapped in the greatest love there is in our universe. That kind of love is unending, and it can only grow in your heart when you share it with others."

Grief always comes as an uninvited guest in your heart, but don't allow it to take up permanent residence; that space is where divine love has made its home. Just like your eyes need a little time to adjust to the darkness before you'll see any light, your heart will also need time with sorrow before it will see happiness again—this is the beauty of life, this is the process of life, this *is* life.

Take comfort in knowing you are never a lone island in the sea of life. Rather, you are a beautiful oasis surrounded by an ocean of divine love—now and forever.

Letting go of grief is never about letting go of your loved one. It's about creating more room in your heart for the love you have for them. If you have great grief, then you must have a very large heart, and that heart needs to be filled with this love so you can endlessly share it with everyone.

When sorrow comes knocking on your door, you don't need to pray for a miracle. Just ask the Lord for enough strength to carry on, enough faith to accept the plan laid out for you, and enough love to lift your spirit through your difficult time. The miracle happens each time you face your grief with divine conviction in your heart.

The greatest part of living is that you can never see the beautiful picture God has created for you, because you are standing on the blueprint. Trust the plan—even when it seems to not make any sense. There will be times when it doesn't, especially when someone is taken from you. It's up to you to seek peace.

So how do you transcend grief?

You'll be in shock, disbelief and denial when you first learn of a loved one's passing, especially if it's sudden or unexpected. How do you cope or get through this? You'll feel like nothing is in your control, and it's not. Our fate may not be in our hands, but our faith through divine love is. Hold this faith in your hands and open your heart to this unending love, for that is where hope is born.

Next, guilt may set in. What could you have done to prevent the tragedy from happening? You'll agonize over what you did or didn't say to your loved one. Your thoughts may become consumed with regret, to the point where you feel guilty feeling happy. It's a time when you'll be vulnerable to self-medicating with drugs and alcohol to dull the unending pain.

When the shadows of sadness darken your heart, reach out to your family and friends. Each one will bring a small ray of hope to your life. Even the smallest candle can brighten a darkened room. Your family and friends truly love you, and they are willing to help you get through this darkest hour. It's perfectly okay to rely on them. You're human. Although it may seem that those closest to you have abandoned you, they have not. It's human to try to retract from pain. When you're grieving, people seem to avoid you. This is the time to be open with your feelings and ask them to, at the very least, just listen to you. Ask for help.

If you don't make it through this pain, anger may set in. You may lash out at those who are closest to you. This is when emotion that's been bottled up within you may bubble over. It's okay to release this emotion, and it's probably healthy to do it, as long as you don't push those you need most away from you. If you feel regret for something you said or did, it's not your fault. Forgive yourself.

When I was a child, my mother once told me, "When

something bad happens to you, share it with as many people as you can, so each one can get rid of a small piece of that sadness. When something good happens to you, hold it in for a while so it will grow. That way, you will have a lot more goodness to go around."

Take comfort in small happiness wins during this period. It's okay to allow yourself to be happy, if only for brief periods. It's all a part of dealing with the variety of the emotions you may be filled with when you feel love is lost. Sadness, loneliness, abandonment, anger, heartache, hatred, and, the other big D: depression, are just a few. The truth is, love never leaves you. You may have just turned away from it. Love always surrounds you, because it lives in the hearts of your community, family, and friends.

After the anger, you will reflect. You may seem lost, or you may wish to be isolated during this time. It's not the big things that will cause you to break down, but the seemingly little insignificant ones. Take time for yourself during this period. Others may seem to be moving on with their life and probably expect you to do the same. However, this is your true grieving time, and it's also a time to plan to move forward with your loss. Know that you are never alone in your sorrow. There is always someone who cares about you. We are all connected in what you're going through, and love is the unending tie.

Finally, you reach acceptance and the light of hope. It's all you can ask for. Your life may still change on a dime. If you take a turn for the worse, will you spend your time suffering in grief or will you accept the divine plan God has for you? Love is paper on which God's blueprint is drafted. If you're having trouble navigating your life without your loved one, chart your course for God's grace, take a step in love's direction and you'll always find your way home.

While attending a conference for veterans I gave a short inspirational speech to a small group of the attendees. Shortly after I finished a woman approached me and said, "I really needed to hear what you said today, especially when you spoke about keeping faith. I have all but lost mine. My brother died in the prime of his life—leaving my entire family reeling in pain. Then, I lost my sister-in-law and niece."

As I was to find out, this was only the beginning of the pain she'd endured.

She reached into her purse and handed me a folded paper funeral program. "My sister-in-law and niece were the pillars of our family. They did the best they could to pick up the pieces after my brother passed away. He died much too young. His sudden passing shocked our family...and now this. They were our family's shining lights. I still can't believe they're all gone in just this short time."

Her eyes glazed over and she stood motionless. "You probably don't know, but earlier this year, my sister-in-law and niece were both murdered in a horrible domestic violence incident involving my niece's estranged boyfriend. God, I miss them all. After my brother passed away, I always thought he would watch over them from heaven, you know—be there to protect and save them, not let something like this happen to them. I have to say that my faith has been shaken to its core. I don't know what to believe anymore. Maybe you can help me make sense of this?"

I pondered her words for several moments, taking in the gravity of the situation and said, "I'm not sure this will ever make sense. In the past I thought that saving someone simply meant to help extend their life. In medical terms, it is just that, but in the eyes of God, saving someone is bringing their soul into divine light. Did you ever consider that your brother *is* truly watching over them, and that the saving occurs on the other side?"

She suddenly breathed a small sigh of relief and hugged me. "You know... I never considered that. I never thought of it that way. You're right."

She pulled back from me slowly, nodding her head in affirmation with her lips pursed, then smiled slightly. "Thank you for telling me this. Somehow I'm finding peace."

I know you don't want to lose someone close to you, and you certainly don't want a loved one to suffer, but death is an inescapable part of life. You will be on the *other side* eventually, we all will. It could be tomorrow or years from now. What really matters is how much kindness and love you share between this day and your last. When the darkest of shadows descends upon you, you need to remember that those shadows always have a higher light source behind them. It's up to you to turn around to see that light.

Family members or friends that have crossed over can then guide you through the rest of your life. When my parents passed, I rejoiced in the fact that two of my greatest fans were now universal guides for me. Know that you are connected forever by the threads of unending love, and those bonds can never be broken.

You may feel that you can't see your deceased loved ones, but they are present in everything around you. You may say you can no longer talk to them, but your words are heard. You may cry because they can't touch you, but they already have within them each gentle whisper of love still residing in your heart. Your pain will ultimately pale in comparison to the joy this unconditional love brings to your precious soul.

———∞———

All flowers wilt. All tears eventually dry. All colors fade in the setting sun, but unconditional love endures forever in the hearts of everyone you've touched with your beautiful soul. To have shared this love—for even a second—is to know God's grace.

You can always find faith within any fear, hope within any loss, and love within any sorrow. Where God is concerned, there is no beginning and end. Your soul is, always has been and always will be, part of this unending Divine light—love in its purest essence.

What could be more beautiful than that?

DECODES

Rely on Grace:

Where there is grace, there is God. Wherever there is faith, there is belief. Where there is love there is hope for God's grace. Above all else, God's unending grace is ever-present for you, but it's up to you to ask for it. It's easy to give up your faith. It takes great courage to keep it during the worst of times.

Seek Small Moments:

You can only be in the present when you fully enjoy the smallest moments of life. Look for the little flashes of love throughout the day. This could be as simple as seeing the beauty in a small child's smile or a fleeting happy thought. Write them down during the day and review them before you go to sleep.

Be Still:

If you find a quiet moment each day, you will also find God within the peacefulness of your thoughts.

Waves of Grief

Why were we separated by this ocean of agonizing time?

When the angels called for your beauty my body could only fall upon the earth that reclaimed you. I grabbed the sand in anger and it spilled from my fingers as you slipped from my life.

Alone in the blackness of a starless night, I could only call upon grief's dark cloak to cover my shivering soul. Time's essence passed as an endless sea of sorrow that washed over me.

Every unbearable wave that broke upon my shore carried but a few of my tears out to that desolate abyss.

When the tempest finally passed, a single light appeared upon the horizon. I wiped the raindrops from my eyes and raised my chin. The rays of this new day gently caressed my cheek. It was love...yes...precious love.

It was then I left the comfort of the shore. I waded among the glistening waves. It was then I realized you were swimming in that same great expanse.

SEEK MIRACLES

"Take pause for the little things in life, for that is where all of love's most precious moments are captured, to glow forever within your heart."—Robert Clancy

●

With every "climb" you undertake in this life—whether it's to get to a better place or simply to clear an obstacle—always pause to take in the divine views, for that's where life's precious miracles are found.

Raising your level of awareness allows you to become hyperconscious and receptive to these beautiful slices of time. It takes effort to release your day-to-day stress, but whenever you do, you'll be free to focus on your greater surroundings. Peace is found in those boundless vistas when you rise above your seemingly chaotic life.

The universe is God's canvas, and we're simply meant to paint it with our unique expression of love. Parts of the picture may be clear to us, but it's often confusing. Just know that the image painted just for you is always clear to God. Trust in the artistry of this unconditional love.

Miracles happen every day—recognizing them is simply a matter of your awareness. It is a miracle every time a child smiles, every time the sun's rays warm your face, every time you share a bit of your heart with someone in need.

Will your soul be ready to experience this beauty the next time a miracle happens in your presence?

———∞———

It was a beautiful Sunday afternoon in July and my wife and I decided to pick up a pizza for dinner on our way home from an event. The pizzeria was located in an area of the city that had seen better days. Many of the apartments and houses were built in the latter half of the nineteenth century. Even though most of the buildings were sun-bleached and covered with peeling paint, I enjoyed the architecture. I often imagined what structures must have looked like when they were first built, and wondered about the people who first lived in them.

"You wait here, I'll run in and get the food. I've got cash," my wife said as she jumped out and closed the car door behind her.

I smiled, and gave her a thumbs-up as she crossed in front of me. I immediately jumped into my office email on my iPhone, looking ahead and hoping to put out any work issues before work began on Monday morning.

The pizza must not have been ready, because she was in the restaurant for longer than usual. I was in the midst of replying to an email when a loud noise caught my attention. I lifted my head and noticed that a stocky, bearded man in his thirties, wearing a football jersey and long sport shorts, had emerged from an apartment building across the street. He was pushing a small, rusted lawnmower that would periodically backfire.

Lost in my thoughts, I absent-mindedly watched him go back and forth across the tiny yard. Suddenly, the mower engine cut out. At first, I thought the engine stalled, or that he hit a rock, because he was gently brushing the grass with his foot adjacent to the mower.

"What the heck is he doing?"

The man knelt down next to the mower, placed his hand on the ground, and cupped both hands as if he was carrying water as he stood up. Suddenly, a small green object leapt from his hands and he fumbled forward to retrieve it.

I started to chuckle. "Oh, he stopped the mower for a frog." It was humorous to see this burly guy chase down the little critter.

Once he secured the frog in his hands, he walked up the road, beyond his house.

"Where the heck is he going?" Quickly looking around, I assumed he was going to toss the frog into the woods behind the house.

To my surprise, he didn't throw the frog. He gently knelt down, carefully placed the frog on the ground in a fern patch, and watched it for a minute to ensure it was safe. Once the frog disappeared into the woods, he walked back to his yard and started his mower. This man had no idea that I had just witnessed his act of compassion. I looked around to see if anyone else had seen what had just happened, but I was the only one. I felt honored. What an incredible reverence for life.

My wife appeared next to our car with a pizza box in her hands. "Sorry for the delay. I was going to come out and get you. They were a little backed up in there, but it's fresh."

I just smiled and said, "I'm really glad there was a delay. I just witnessed one of those precious life moments."

She looked at me quizzically, but said nothing as I turned on the engine and drove away with the smell of pizza wafting in the car.

———⟨∞⟩———

Wherever you plant the seeds of kindness—whether with words or deeds—your feet will always walk the fertile ground of unconditional love. Your basket will always be filled with a bounty of faith, and only hope will ever reign over you.

A miracle is found in every smile, every act of kindness, and every ounce of love. When you lead with love, you'll end standing upon mountains of grace. Is your view clear enough?

Decodes

Develop Reverence

Be awe-inspired by the grace that surrounds you. Take a moment each day, and look for the little miracles. They can happen anywhere, and most of the time when you least expect them. When you begin to see life through the eyes of grace, you will only have incredible views containing the vistas of faith, love, and hope.

Create Small Miracles

If you want to create a small miracle today, make a child smile. You can't expect miracles to just happen. You need to create them every time you smile, share a hug, or simply brighten someone's day with a kind word.

Be Welcome

Being divine in nature is not enough. You must act upon this goodness with every fiber of your being. It's not just thankfulness that matters, but also welcoming. When you are welcoming, the abundance of the Universe will fill your mind, body, and soul with goodness.

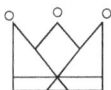

PRINCESS
CHRISTINE'S STORY

"It seems that there's always someone who can find fault with even the greatest piece of artwork. So, when someone finds fault with you, just know you're a masterpiece of God's work." — Robert Clancy

E ach of us has a negative tape from our childhood that can play over and over in our mind. This could be a hurtful label or incident that affects your self-worth, but also one that impedes your growth and potential. Inadequacies with your psyche can plague you to the point that you never feel worthy of your own happiness. You deserve happiness! Why rob yourself of it?

The past is just that—past. Letting go of previous negativity frees your heart to pursue a hope-filled future. Don't live in a past that no longer exists, or a worry-filled future that may never come to pass. Live for the love you have in the now.

It's so easy to fall into these negative thought patterns and overlook the wonderful things that make you a beautiful soul. When you look in the mirror and you fail to see the special person you truly are, remember the grace deep within you. Your true friends and your family only see this gracious image of you. All the healing serenity you'll ever need is housed within your heart, and you are always a welcomed visitor there. It's up to you to knock on that door.

It takes courage to face your fears; it requires faith, hope, and love to conquer them, but it's up to you to declare the war. Fear shouldn't be held prisoner in the basement of your consciousness; release it so you too can be free. There will be times when you need to pass through the darkest shadows in the valley of your greatest fears and doubts. As you struggle through, know that every movement forward brings you one step closer to the grace that resides atop the mountain of hope overseeing that vale.

The sacred peace from which your soul is made is a place for healing, love and guidance. Listen to it, and know you're never alone. Divine guidance doesn't come from speaking to God through prayer, it comes from listening to Him with the stillness of your soul.

The true power of perspective is achieved when you're able to visualize how something bad in your life could have been much worse; and you're thankful for everything you're still blessed with. Your physical well-being is directly connected to your outlook, and it needs to be a positive one. When your mind focuses on the positive side, you'll only embody a soulful happiness.

—⚮—

I opened the passenger door of the sedan and slid into the seat with my hands clenched as tight as my teeth. "Mom, are you sure this is the *right* dress shop for me? The dresses they sell there are… um…you know…upscale and a bit on the *small side*."

"Relax. You'll be fine. I'm sure we'll find a wedding dress that'll fit you. They carry larger sizes too."

Not exactly the reassuring words I wanted to hear. The taunts from the first boy I ever kissed were endlessly echoing in my mind. Instead of the fairytale day my mother planned for me, all I could visualize was the sneer on that boy's face as he delivered a fatal spear deep into my soul.

"You're such a whale. Man the harpoons!"

As I covered my face with my hands, other boys on the playground quickly surrounded me. "We're gonna need a bigger ship to reel in this whale. Look at her...she's such a cow!"

I was a circus sideshow—an elephant in the center ring. *"Why me? Why would he do this to me?"*

Beginning with that horrific day and all throughout my high school years I was endlessly teased about my body image. By today's standards, I was beautiful. I just didn't fit the ideal model body type of the time—super thin. I would never again see a reflection of the strong, athletic, Romanesque, curvy Marilyn Monroe beauty I was. I was broken. I was worthless. I hated mirrors from the neck down.

Planning my wedding was an exhilarating time for me, full of love, hope and possibility, but being the glamorous center of attention terrified me to my core. I'd spent years just trying to fit in among my peers. Never to be the boyfriend-toting popular girl, but to be the strong, smart, athletic one in the group.

I braced myself at the entrance to the store. "Oh my God! I'm a size sixteen going to the most exclusive wedding boutique in town. Shopping for clothes...looking at myself in the mirror... this is not my thing!"

My mother nudged my shoulder toward the bridal salon located in the back of the store. "Come on dear. This is gonna to be fun. It's time to beautify you."

I cowered away from her hand and tried to blend in. My best efforts to shrivel into the rug failed. *"Okay. I know where the dresses are."*

Suddenly a voice rang out from the side of the store, and a middle-aged woman emerged from behind a rack of dresses.

"Can I help you? What are we looking for today?"

Her perfume was almost as nauseating as her perky attitude.

"Wedding gowns for a bride-to-be," my mother said.

She paused to survey me from head to toe with her pearly white teeth gleaming. "Oh wonderful! I think I can help with that. We have a few selections that may work for her size. This way ladies and let's get started. Shall we?" *She knew this was going to be a challenge.*

The bridal gown viewing area was a circular room engulfed in mirrors with a pedestal at its epicenter. Shimmering white wedding dresses lined the racks surrounding the viewing area. For a minute I was excited, until I noticed that they only seemed to carry petite sizes. I felt outclassed—so small on the inside, and so very big on the outside. I wanted to run out of the store.

"Come. This is your day to be a princess," my mother beckoned.

I froze for a second, but her reassuring smile made me push forth into the bridal arena.

Sensing my apprehension and a possible lost sale, the sales rep chirped, "We have several elegant choices I'm sure you'll love. You'll look beautiful, dear. I guarantee it."

I didn't believe her. "*Great*. I can't wait to jump into the middle of this funhouse of mirrors. I won't even be able to get my arms into these pixie dresses."

"What was that?"

"Never mind. Um...where are your other gown sizes...*the larger ones?*"

She pursed her lips trying to keep her plastic smile on. "Oh dear. Our in-store selections are a bit limited in that area, but any of these garments can be altered."

I know that selecting the perfect wedding dress is no easy task for any bride-to-be, but I felt like a duck out of water—an ugly duck. Dress after dress just didn't fit my body type.

"Do they have any dresses for *normal* people?" my mother mumbled, as she shuffled through another dozen gowns.

"Is that supposed to make me feel good? Can we do this another day?"

"I'll be able to find you a dress. Can you just be patient?"

After trying to squeeze into dozens of dresses two sizes too small for me, I finally slumped into a viewing chair and let out a sigh of frustration. "Just let me know if you find anything."

My mother was determined, and kept sifting through their collections for another thirty minutes. "What a precious dress," my mother said as she held the white glimmering splendor out for all to see. "This is exquisite, and I think it's your size."

It was a wonderful piece, full of shimmering beads and delicate lace—truly beautiful.

"It just might fit too," I thought. "It'll be tight, but it just might be close enough for a seamstress to make the alterations. Please be the one." I crossed my fingers.

I quickly grabbed the garment and held it against my body to size it up. For that fleeting moment, I felt lacy hope in my hands. My eyes were beaming with anticipation. "Mom. This could be the one! I can't wait to try it on."

A few minutes later, I emerged from the changing booth shattered. The gown was awkwardly hanging off of me. Although the arms fit, it was too snug in the shoulders to close up the back, and my bra was completely exposed. My mother and the saleswoman swooped in to try to clumsily hold the dress closed with their hands and I broke down into tears, absolutely humiliated. Cue the circus music. It was at that very moment that a tiny angelic voice pieced the sorrowful air.

"Look Mommy, *it's Cinderella!*"

I quickly spun around to find a petite blond-haired girl pointing at me. As I gazed into her gleaming blue eyes, a big smile washed across her cherub-like face. It was the glass slipper my soul needed, and the one I still wear in my heart today.

—⬿—

The most honest words you'll ever hear are spoken by children. Listen to their truth with all your heart. When you see life through their eyes, you will finally begin to see your own life re-emerge again.

Decodes

Rescue your Inner Child

Your innocence from childhood is never lost unless you allow it to be. Shine bright by turning on your *young star* within.

Stay Positive

Attitude truly is everything, especially when that outlook on your life comes from deep within your soul. Each time you have a negative thought replace it with at least two positive ones. Whatever you're struggling with, you can and will make it past it if you believe in the divine light within your heart.

Change Your Perspective

Changing your perspective about an unpleasant situation is not about changing your mind on the matter. It's about empowering your heart to rise above it.

You're a Special Soul

Did you know you're a beautiful masterpiece of celestial art?

God sculpted your body, painted your portrait, and forged your soul from stardust.

An angel's breath was used to create your smile. Every element of the universe is fused into your delicate soul; the most important is the Divine love placed gently into your heart.

As with any masterwork, you may weather with age or get damaged a bit along the way, but doesn't that add to your beauty and mystique?

Don't ever change who you are.

You're loved and cherished in heaven just the way you are.

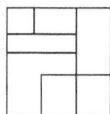

Right Angles

"Grief isn't about an ending of love...it's about the beginning of understanding how deep your love truly is."— Robert Clancy

❀

L ife is simply a series of changes—some difficult, some wonderful, but isn't that what the beauty of life is all about? It's true that you never know what lies ahead for you and those around you. Each of your days can be marked with many twists and turns, some of which are seemingly for the worse.

I've learned that you just need to trust the ocean of change to be able to successfully sail upon the ebbs and flows of these disruptive waves. As you experience these changes, know that change is a constant the universe, but also know that love is the one thing in the universe that changes everything. You are not born better.

You can only become better through the challenges you face with faith, love and precious hope.

———∞———

As she answered the phone, my wife's face turned ashen white. "Oh no, this can't be true. What can we do? Do you need anything?"

I knew this wasn't good.

"Yes, he's here. I'll let you speak to him in a second. How did it happen? How are you holding up? I'm so sorry. I don't know what to say."

I was straining to hear her every word, but the clues as to what happened weren't there.

A few days earlier, my father had fallen out of his wheelchair when he tried to stand on his own. "Is my dad okay? Did he have another stroke?" My mind winced.

She slowly walked toward me, extending the phone, "It's your friend Ron. He wants to tell you himself."

My thoughts were spinning as I lifted the phone to my ear. "Ron?" My mind raced as I tried to switch gears from my family to his.

His voice was barley above a whisper. "Hi Bob. You're the first person I've called and I want you to hear this from me before this hits the news. My sister Cindy committed suicide a few hours ago, and she attempted to take the life of her baby, too. I don't have all of the details yet, but by sheer miracle, her son has only a minor scratch. He'll be okay...well at least physically. I pray that he has no memory of this, only happy ones of Cindy."

I was absolutely stunned. Cindy was a bright soul, who was as sharp as she was caring. She ranks up there as one the kindest and smartest people I'd ever known. I always looked up to her, and still do. Not only was Cindy a valedictorian from my high school, but she also attained a perfect score on the Law School Admission Test. This act was so far out of character for her; I didn't know what to think. I tried to respond with something that would make sense, but nothing came. I simply blurted out, "Why?"

Trying to make sense of it himself, I could hear him grit his teeth as his voice raised up, "She wouldn't take her medication. We think it was the postpartum depression she was battling. I can almost understand her doing this to herself, but why her baby? She tried to be a murderer! She failed, and I'm thankful for her finally failing at something!"

"Ron, it's not her fault. Her mind was broken. A person can't fix that on their own. You and I both know that was not our Cindy who did this. We can't change what happened, but maybe we can that do something with this that helps others, in her memory."

At that moment, we both vowed to make a something good come out of this. Our lives were changed. It's one of those right angles in life that takes you by complete surprise, turns your world upside down, and spits you out on the other side.

When the call ended, my wife and I just sat emotionless on our couch, hugging each other.

I'd scoured my mind to try to think of the last time I saw Cindy, and what our last conversation was. I wanted to remember every detail of her face. I wanted to hug her one more time. It was a vivid memory—the Thanksgiving gathering at Ron's house.

It was an awkward encounter. I nearly tripped over a baby in a car seat placed oddly in the middle of the kitchen floor. "Maybe the baby is in here to nap or something."

A few minutes later, Cindy entered the kitchen. An emotionless, blank stare was painted on her face. She slowly leaned against the kitchen counter, and said nothing.

Peering downward, I confusingly motioned, "Is this your new baby boy? I don't think I've been introduced to him yet."

She glanced down at the car seat and then stared past me. "Yeah, that's him. He's not developing correctly."

Before I could respond, she suddenly turned her head in disgust and hastily walked out if the kitchen.

My eyes widened, and my jaw dropped as I knelt down to check on the baby. "What the heck it going on? Maybe she had a stressful ride up. Something is way off."

I surveyed the kitchen for someone to come and bail me out, but the rescue party never arrived.

After what felt like an eternity, Cindy returned to the kitchen. She casually stepped over the infant and into my personal space.

"Tell me about this book you've written," she cross-examined. "I heard it's *supposed* to have a positive message," she continued sarcastically.

I was suddenly a defendant on trial.

"Uh...it's a book I wrote to hopefully inspire others to have more compassion in their lives," I replied stuttering my words. "It's umm...you know..."

Eyeing me down like a hawk ready to swoop down on a field mouse, she stopped me in my tracks with a steely glare. She was a seasoned, well-trained lawyer who could argue any point with the best of them. I was definitely unarmed in this battle of wits.

"You don't think that will make any difference, do you? That's a complete waste of time," she retorted as she stormed out of the kitchen.

The whole incident was so odd, I never said anything about it to anyone. I just spent the rest of my time at the party avoiding her. It's what you naturally do when you encounter something negative or painful. You defensively retract or recoil in fear. I wish I had said something, but what do you do when you are so caught off guard?

In the weeks and months following Cindy's passing, we came to find she was suffering from *postpartum psychosis*, a rare psychiatric condition in which symptoms of high mood swings, racing thoughts, depression, severe confusion, loss of inhibition, paranoia, hallucinations and delusions set in, beginning suddenly in the weeks to months after childbirth.

The symptoms vary greatly and can change quickly. [1] Cindy was at the extreme end of this affliction.

After something so terrible as this, you're left thinking, "What could I have done to prevent this? Could I have comforted them? Why didn't I see the signs? Didn't they know I love them?"

There are no easy answers. When someone commits suicide, it leaves such a black hole in your life. You struggle to understand the anguish the person was going through; one so desperate that their only escape was death. Cindy, unfortunately,

If Cindy was susceptible to suicide, then we're all at risk. It's a thought that has not left my mind since that day.

In the months following Cindy's death, I caught a news story about a seven-year-old boy who was visiting an army hospital with his mother. The boy saw the word "Suicide" on a prevention poster aimed at its service members.

He didn't know what the word was, so he pointed to it and asked him mother, "Mommy, what's that 'S' word?"

His mother pretended not to hear him, and started walking faster in hopes that she could avoid the difficult explanation.

The boy pressed his mother again about the meaning of the word, so she explained to him what suicide means, and how some soldiers experience injuries that aren't on the outside. Trying not to upset her son, she explained, "When they don't have any broken arms or legs and no blood. You can't see the sadness inside them."

Troubled by the idea of someone taking his or her own life, the boy asked for a marker and post-it notes. His message was poignant. He simply wrote the words *"ask...for...help...!!!!"* Each word and the exclamation points were written on a separate post-it note and posted onto the wall in the hospital. His inspirational message of hope moved hospital officials so much, they displayed it for everyone to see. [2]

Each of us may have our own unique dance steps, but we should always be mindful that we're all dancing on the same great dance floor of life. We just need to be there for each other. It's that simple.

—⦵—

There is always someone there for you. There is always someone who loves you just as you are. There is always someone you can lean on for help.

When you cry in solitude, you weep alone. When you cry in the rain, your tears mix with droplets from heaven and those tears are always touching another person somewhere else.

Know that you are never alone in your sorrow. Someone cares about you. We are all connected, and love is our unending tie. Don't ever let go.

For more information on postpartum depression and psychosis, please visit Postpartum Support International at postpartum.net

1. Jones, I; Chandra, PS; Dazzan, P; Howard, LM (15 November 2014). "Bipolar disorder, affective psychosis, and schizophrenia in pregnancy and the post-partum period.". Lancet. 384 (9956): 1789–99.

2. Victoria Cavaliere NEW YORK DAILY NEWS, Thursday, February 7, 2013. http://www.nydailynews.com/news/national/boy-7-sticky-note-message pleading suicide-article-1.1258066

Decodes

Be Aware of Others

The greatest perception you can have is when you're aware of the love in another's heart. Everyone is dealing with some issue in their life, when you can be a helping hand, a kind word or simply a shoulder to rest upon, you've done your job.

Weather Life's Storms

The mighty oak tree knows its strength comes from its roots—it's the only way it weathers all of life's storms, grows taller in the face of adversity, and no matter what, it will always reach for the light. Anything you're going through at the moment will always be a distant memory in the future. It may be hard to weather some of life's storms, but you can do it with the help of your family and friends.

Stand for Love

You could stand up to shout in protest against something you disagree with, but quite often it is the quiet heart that speaks louder than anger ever could.

PERSPECTIVE

"When life seems to be taking you for a ride, know that divine love will always ultimately be the final destination. Trust in the lessons of the journey. Believe in the truth discovered in your purpose."— Robert Clancy

Have you ever had one of those days where everything just goes wrong, and no matter what you do, it just seems to get worse? I see you nodding your head. You know exactly what I'm talking about. You're probably thinking - *Yep! That sums up the last year of my life!*

When you keep pushing on something, only to experience more setbacks, that's God's way of telling you to change your pathway, or just let it be for now. Your attention is desired elsewhere. Trust your intuition to find that other pathway. A door closed in your face is not a loss; it just means there's an open window somewhere else for you. All you need to do is spread your wings, and fly in that new direction.

I've always found that after something seemingly terrible happens to me—bad news, a setback, or even a health issue—I've always discovered something positive within those situations that far outweighs any perceived negativity. This is the silver lining, or more so the *divine perspective* we all need to seek.

Within every one of life's problems, resides its solution. All you need to do is change your perspective on the matter to see it. Changing your viewpoint about an unpleasant situation is not just about changing your mind on the matter; it's about empowering your soul to rise infinitely above it.

———∞———

A couple of years ago, I was asked to speak to a group of people recovering at my regional hospital. To my surprise, they were all in the suicide-watch lockdown ward and they were young—between the ages of eighteen and twenty-five. What I immediately noticed about this group was how vibrant and full of life they all seemed to be. At first, I couldn't fathom that any one of them was suicidal, until they shared their stories.

One particular young man shared that he attempted to take his life because his father had recently passed away.

With tears streaming down his cheeks, he slowly lifted his head. "How am I supposed to go on without him? He's my best friend in this world. I don't know how to survive without him."

His incredible love for his father was evident. I paused for a moment, and asked him a question to which I'd already surmised the answer. "Do you have children of your own?"

One of his hands slowly slid along his IV pole, while his other hand wiped the tears from his eyes. "No, I don't have kids. I'm not even married."

I looked straight into his eyes and smiled. "Don't you want to be the father your dad was to you to your *future* children?"

He shook his head in affirmation, as if he'd been shocked back to life. "Wow! I never thought about that. You're so right. My dad lives within me, and that's what I can pass on to my own kids someday. How did I never see this?"

His new lease on life...*perspective.*

———∞———

Within every one of life's problems is its solution; you just have to change your heart's perspective on the matter to see it.

Life is nothing more than a series of highs and lows, but it's designed that way so that when you're at those summits, you can enjoy the majestic view of those valleys.

When the challenges of life cause so much pain that life itself becomes too much to bear, know that there's always a silver lining awaiting you. Allow the love from your family and friends to carry you through those dark hours. There truly is a light at the end of every dark tunnel. You're never alone.

DECODES

Take Time To Heal

When you can't...then just let it be. When you have hope, you have all the time you'll ever need to complete your healing process.

Pain is Shared

We're all going through something in this life. Don't let your pain be what defines you. Instead, let it be what helps find you. Dig deep within your heart, and you'll discover that everything you need to get through the tough times is and always has been within you.

Stay Strong and Hold On

I know it's a cliché to say "stay strong," but I also know a mighty oak tree knows its strength comes from its roots. It's the only way it weathers all the storms, grows taller in the face of adversity, and no matter what, it will always reach for the light. You can only know your true strength when you've been tested.

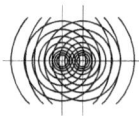

DETOX

"Negative people may be attracted to your light, like moths to a flame in the night. A butterfly, on the other hand, spreads its beautiful wings and sails effortlessly in the light. It's just better to rise above any darkness you encounter."— Robert Clancy

❖

My wife and I have a favorite saying from Maya Angelou we use when we're dealing with a failing friendship or business relationship: "When someone shows you who they are, believe them the first time."

Whether you perceive someone to be "good" or "bad," trust your gut instinct about whether they are a positive or negative influence on your life. The higher your vibration is, the less you will choose cancerous relationships. It's perfectly fine to remove yourself from friendships that are no longer worthy of your time—from people who are using and abusing your goodwill.

Where does negativity stem from in your life? Does negativity surround some friendships that have lost their luster? Right now, you're probably thinking, "I know exactly who that is!" And, you're correct!

Carefully evaluate each relationship you have—they're all part of you. If a bond is not uplifting your soul, your family, or your life's mission, it may be time to cut your losses and walk away—and that's okay. The worst thing you can do is nothing at all. It's always better to make a choice rather than be mired in indecision. Make an informed decision, then act with love in your heart. Choose life. Choose love. Choose your own happiness.

We all make mistakes and poor judgment calls that bring people into our lives who potentially drag us down. It's human nature. It's not that people are *bad*, they're just not right for us at this time in our lives. To accurately see another for who they are, look past what your eyes see. Drop your preconceptions. Look deeply with your heart.

You can't go back and fix your past mistakes, but you can move forward with love and forgiveness. If you do, issues of the past will become a distant memory.

While I was a young child, my mother and father taught me the old adage, "Birds of a feather flock together." What they were teaching me is that you become whomever you surround yourself with. The same is true for your soul. You are what you encircle your heart with. Negative people can deeply affect your outlook, growth, and life path. Attitude is everything— especially when the view of your life comes from the depths of your soul.

If opposites attract, that would explain why you occasionally have negative people around you. Never mind them, and just move while you keep on radiating your beautiful positive energy.

—⊗—

Shortly after graduating college, I ended a long friendship that was embroiled in negativity. This departure was from someone I wholeheartedly supported up until discoveries about the darker side of his life were brought to light. He outwardly presented himself as a caring and gregarious leader, but there was always this enigmatic side to him. I discovered this elusive part of his personality contained a licentious lifestyle that he was hiding. To be his friend, I had chosen to overlook or ignore the signs. But, deep down inside I always felt something was off.

The unraveling of our friendship began with an unsubstantiated rumor about him being a womanizer and illicit drug user. A mutual acquaintance of ours contacted me privately with allegations of improper conduct, and shared some salacious details. When I first heard these allegations, I nearly laughed them off. It just didn't add up. But, even though this was completely unsubstantiated hearsay, I was now entangled with this downward spiral of negativity, due to our close friendship.

When I first confronted him about these shocking claims, he said, "You know me. I'm a good guy. This woman is just trying to bring me down." He carefully and convincingly painted his accuser as a vindictive individual, bent on revenge.

"I was dating her and broke it off because she's not my type. She's just jealous because I don't want a relationship with her. She's obviously trying to get back at me," he said.

I believed him. How could I not? Everything else I knew about him was positive. This unproven claim just didn't make sense at the time. I was angry that I was involved in this rumor, but chose to support him. Yet, something deep inside me didn't sit quite right. I should have trusted my gut, but chose instead to simply ignore that "little voice" inside me, hoping the situation would simply go away.

Several months later, more rumors of his insidious behavior surfaced. This time was different—now there were mutual friends making these claims. I again confronted him, and received the same rationalization he showered me with before. After pressing him with some of the evidence I had at hand, he final broke and admitted his guilt. The truth sent me reeling.

How did I not see through this?

I was now faced with that difficult crossroads decision. Do I keep this person in my life to try to help him, or do I drop him now? I felt like I was dealing with a *Dr. Jekyll and Mr. Hyde.* I needed more time to sort it all out. His issues had already infiltrated our circle of friends. This situation was a complete detriment to my life path that had seemingly come out of nowhere. I was angry—that deep, gritty anger that comes from the core of my stomach. *The signs were there. Why didn't I believe them and respond earlier?*

After I had felt I had gained enough clarity about the situation, I decided to confront him at a neutral location. This is where I found a perfect opportunity to pull him aside.

"I really can't be associated with anyone who lacks the moral fiber you've displayed. What you've done goes against everything I stand for. You're on a destructive path that leads either to jail, or an early death," I said with conviction. "Do you realize how many people you've hurt with your incredibly selfish behavior?"

He seemed lost, and just looked at the ground. For several moments, he didn't respond. Then he raised his head slightly, but didn't make eye contact with me.

Another sign, for sure.

In a low, grievous tone, he said, "You're right. Let me make this up to you. I will be that person who you will be proud of again. I'll get the counseling and help I need, but I need you to be there for me."

It was everything I wanted to hear. It was everything he knew I *needed* to hear. My intuition knew better, but I gave him another chance. In the weeks that followed, I gathered the puzzle pieces of his shattered life, but the picture that emerged didn't look good. It became clear that he was clever at masking indiscretions, and he'd been getting away with this behavior for several years.

A few months passed and, to my surprise, the situation appeared to be getting better. During that time, he would periodically share that his counseling sessions were going well and he was making progress. Then, *wham!* Right back to square one. I learned he was never in counseling, and he was selling drugs to support his habit. Although his actions were a cry for help, he refused any assistance I or anyone else offered.

This has all been just lip service to gain my support. He's just been surrounding himself with good people to facilitate his illusion of having a good reputation. I was absolutely incensed. This additional betrayal was more than I was willing to accept in our friendship.

A few days after learning about these latest allegations, I asked him to meet me for breakfast. My intention was to end our friendship. At that moment, I had a huge realization— I didn't need to unleash my host of unbridled feelings on him, I just needed to acknowledge his life path with love, while recognizing that it was now different from mine.

Over breakfast, he offered me more empty assurances: "It will be different this time. I can change to make you proud of me." But I was done with the friendship. I was able to finally just let go.

"I hope you understand that we're on different roads and I need to move on. I hope someday you'll get the help you need. I realize I can't change what you do with your life...I can only change what I do with mine."

As I walked to my car, I felt free. I had released him with love. While I drove back to my apartment, I reflected upon the impact he had had on my life. Although there were many positive highlights surrounding our friendship, nearly every negative experience over the preceding years was also connected to him. The disruptive strife he brought was a huge hole in my life path. I also came to the realization that this person was not going to change, and I needed to accept that with love. It was not in my control; it was not my job. As much as I wished to help him, he was not willing to accept it.

Once I closed this chapter of my life completely, new doors opened to me that I would have never realized had this relationship not ended. My heart and mind were clear.

——∞——

The best way to end a relationship is to do so with honesty. Speaking your truth does set you free. If nothing else, be honest and truthful with yourself. What you say from the heart is equally as valuable as how you say it. Let your words ring with kindness and compassion.

In retrospect, I had to take responsibility for giving this person access to my life, family, and friends. The signs were always there. Why didn't I respond earlier? To what parts of this negative situation did I contribute? These were dilemmas I had to face and contemplate over time.

Ultimately, I learned that if your life seems enveloped in negativity, there must be only love *just* outside of that. If you walk with all the faith you have toward the glimmers of that love, you'll find the shadows of darkness that had surrounded you were only an illusion all along.

DECODES

Evaluate Negativity

Ignoring negative people in your life creates tension you don't need. Speak directly to them about your feelings, and move on if necessary. Most people won't change, and this is not your fault, it is not even your responsibility. The only thing you are responsible for is yourself and what you put into the relationship.

Trust Your Gut

Your intuition is one of the best compasses you have. Trust it! Your mind can evaluate and process information faster than any computer on the planet. All this information goes into your subconscious. You are constantly reading and processing subtle life clues. If something is gnawing at you, there's a reason.

It Could Be You

Ask yourself honestly: Are you facilitating negative relationships in your life? Take an authentic inventory and change your negative patterns.

Seek new opportunities. During a nasty storm, it's okay to duck and cover. All storms eventually pass, blue skies return, and the sun shines again. This is when you need to face the devastation left in the wake of a storm, and start rebuilding. When you begin anew, there is always an opportunity to make things better than they were before.

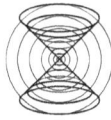

PRESENCE

"May your day begin with a beautiful sunrise; may your year end with happiness and smiles; may your life always know the love and importance of family."

— *Robert Clancy*

❋

Gratitude is more than just giving thanks; it's giving all the love in your heart to those who are dear to you and all the beauty in your life. It's true that most find the holidays stressful, especially when finances are tight, but as stressful as it may be to coordinate that dinner or have guests at your house, time spent with family is priceless. You never know who might not be sitting at your holiday gathering next year.

This past January, one of my childhood best friends passed away. A little over two years ago, my beautiful niece suddenly succumbed to complications with type-1 diabetes while attending her second semester at college. In recent years, both my mother and father have passed.

My niece and mother had infectious smiles continuously painted upon their faces that would always light up our holidays. My father's sense of humor was a staple dish with dinner, too. After grace he would always ask, "Who's hungry?" followed with "Well...look in the mirror and get fed up." We'd all smirk, shake our heads and say, "Good one Pop!" To which he'd reply, "I'll pop yah!" Not having them all with us, especially during the holidays, has left a large void in my family's heart. I know first hand what that kind of grief can do to a family, but my parents raised my siblings and I to be strong, to take life head on, and to always know that our true gifts come from our hearts.

I hope you take this lesson of the heart from my playbook. A loving family will give you strong roots to anchor with, so you may weather any storms of the heart. They'll give you wings for your soul, so you can go places you never imagined.

Life is too precious to live it in sorrow. Let your tears become the droplets from a sun shower. Allow a smile to be your next sunrise. God made your soul from those glimmering stars in the heavens, and you should always shine. The great circle of life is you'll always return to whence you came. Your responsibility is to work on earning your halo while you're here.

Isn't it time to rejoice for the love you all share? Isn't it time to share that loving bond with everyone around you?

The greatest gift you can give this holiday isn't a *present*—it's your *presence*. You may cherish a loving memory from the past, but why not embrace someone right now to create a loving reality.

Do you want to know what the most beautiful gifts this world has? Just open someone's heart with kindness, and you'll know them all. Take pause to enjoy the little things this holiday.

You are the gift!

—∞—

Give thanks...for your family, your friends. The love you all share is your true blessing. Never let go of the beautiful memories you've all shared together. Every one of those memories contains the essence of what love truly is. If you feel like time is slipping through your hands, don't worry...love is what you're supposed to hold onto. Love is the only gift you take with you to heaven.

DECODES

Be the Gift

Love comes in a one-size-fits-all package, so you'll always have something to wear upon your heart. It's very easy to warm someone's heart; you simply have to wrap them in a blanket of your love. Bring that warmth, and be the gift!

Know You're Always Home

Home is where the heart is, especially when you've built that shelter around your family's heart.

Celebrate

Celebrate life, especially yours! You're a beautiful soul bestowed upon the world. Love, laugh, smile, be kind, and share your gifts with everyone around you!

LOST SOULS

*"You may think forgiveness will imprison your pride,
but it will only set your soul free."* — Robert Clancy

●

In one way or another, we've all strayed from God's grace and our soul's path, but in reality, we're never without a Divine compass or a map of heaven to guide us. You always have a choice, but it is never without a greater framework surrounding you, even if you are not consciously aware of it. In the view of the Divine, our soul is never lost, and our life is a journey of choices and possibilities, all leading to the place where we ultimately belong.

God provides for each of us on our journey. It may not always be food and shelter, or what we desire at that moment, but God is always present with unconditional love, understanding, and what we truly need—even though we may not see it.

Whether you're at the foot of the mountain, or at the top, God's grace is the same. It's all a matter of perspective. When you're at the bottom, will you have the faith to climb to the monumental grandeur? When you're at the top, will you share the splendor of God that is before you?

For some, faith is a choice not taken, love is a choice not chosen, and hope is all but forgotten. And that is their perception. But, where God is concerned, faith, love, and hope are forever persistent in everyone and everything.

You don't need to see an angel to know unending love; just bask in the joy of a child's smile. You don't need to visit heaven to know infinite peace, just gaze at the stars above your head on any given night. You don't need to speak with God to know forgiveness, just accept it with all of your heart. When you marvel at your surroundings and everything you're blessed with, you'll find everything you require from God's kingdom is already in yours.

———⟨∞⟩———

I recently spoke with a friend who is struggling with a very difficult situation. She asked me, "How do I forgive?"

I have to admit, I was perplexed. No one had ever asked me that question before, nor had I given it much thought. I've always believed that altering your perspective about an unpleasant situation is not about changing your mind. Rather, it's about empowering your heart to rise above it. Still, this didn't seem to be the complete answer to her question.

Forgiveness starts by first forgiving yourself, so forgive *you* with all of your heart. This is the first hurdle, and so many people fail to clear it for their entire lives. No matter how far you think you've fallen, you can always get back to level ground by lifting your chin up, having faith in each step you take toward the light, and holding God's grace in your heart to overcome any fear.

My dad, a World War II veteran and D-Day invasion survivor, gave me this advice for learning forgiveness: "Be a leader, not a follower, and realize that sometimes you need to lead by following. Above all, be accountable. It's the only way people will respect you." In my leadership development work, I've learned to handle difficult choices and situations with grace, while being responsible for my mistakes.

It takes courage to forgive yourself. It takes caring to apologize to those you hurt, and it takes love to complete the healing process. True love sees no color, no race, no religion, and no creed. Love just accepts you for who you are—a precious spirit with your human flaws.

There isn't a single person who isn't born to make mistakes. This is the nature of being human. However, with each misstep we take, an opportunity is created to learn forgiveness from within. Never judge yourself; that's God's responsibility, and the jury always rules for unconditional love.

The greatest hurdle to clear is forgiving someone else. Many people I've spoken with about this feel that forgiving someone means that you are condoning their actions. It's not. Forgiveness is never about the other person. It's about releasing the pain you've endured, so you can move forward in life with freedom.

Choosing not to forgive allows you to undervalue yourself. You're a sacred heart encased in a precious, beautiful soul capable of sharing life's greatest gift—love.

Never squander that gift.

Forgiveness is a choice.

———⌘———

Every day is filled with God's grace; and every second we have choice to share this divine love with someone else. Forgiveness doesn't take a piece of your heart away...it carries your heart to a place of peace.

Forgiveness will always set at least one person completely free—*you*.

DECODES

Be Accountable

When you're accountable, you can be counted upon.
There are so many people in your life who depend upon
you in one way or another. When they can rely upon you
in any capacity, you make both your life
and theirs stronger.

Accept Your Flaws

Let's face it, no one is perfect and it is perfectly normal to
make mistakes. They key is to learn from them and move
forward in a positive direction.

Accept the Flaws of Others

The road to forgiveness can only be traveled within
your heart. Just follow the signs for love and be open to
accepting the mistakes others make. The big lesson here
is, when you're capable of forgiving yourself, you're
capable of forgiving the faults of others.

GIVING

"Volunteers become immortal when they live on in the hearts of those they've served."— Robert Clancy

I'm often asked, "What's your definition of volunteerism?" Although most people think of the traditional models - such as giving time or money to charitable causes - for me, volunteerism starts the minute you do anything to ease someone's life, even in a simple way, such as sharing your smile or a kind word. There's a profound difference between *'passing on kindness'* and *'passing kindness on.'* Volunteerism starts in your heart, and should be an unending journey of love.

When we join the human race, we seem to be constantly running along the shadows of doubt and fear, but through simple acts of kindness, we can steer ourselves out of the darkness. I firmly believe we're never alone in this race, because we are always held by the higher power. In times of doubt, I remind myself that I can always win this race by simply having faith that every act of kindness matters.

As a parent, I've discovered volunteerism to be a profound way to incorporate learning into our daily family life. I've taught my son from an early age that each day of life is a blank canvas, and there is always a choice on how you will paint it. Will you choose to color it with kindness, compassion, and caring, or will you choose apathy? Helping others provides an educational experience of what love truly is and how to bring this into your entire life—your career, your circle of friends, family, and community. I often tell him, "It's true that if you love your job, you'll never work a day in your life, but imagine if your job was loving - you'd live every day of your life working in happiness."

Many working parents seem too busy to do extracurricular family activities, let alone incorporate learning into their daily routines. Volunteerism provides a perfect way to do both. For example, my son enjoys participating in the Boy Scouts, so I joined his troop as a volunteer Assistant Scoutmaster. Not only does this offer me an opportunity to spend quality time with him, but also a chance to assist him in learning various essential life skills, compassion for others, and a greater appreciation of community, while getting a great education on what it truly means to be a citizen. You can't get this type of learning from a book—you can only experience it by living it.

When volunteerism becomes part of your soul's DNA, it never takes away from life—it becomes what life is meant to be. We're all meant to lead others through our compassion. Never lose sight of the fact that someone always looks up to you.

—◦∞◦—

Sharing is one of the first acts of compassion we learn as a child. In the beginning, it is difficult for us because we don't fully understand the purpose of this precious gesture. It often takes encouragement from others to learn this behavior—a true gift we share with each other. Think of the first time you shared something, or the last time you saw a child do this. Did it warm your heart? Giving always has love attached as its return to sender.

DECODES

Volunteer With Your Passions

What do you love to do as a hobby or in your spare time? Find a way to connect this interest with a volunteer activity. For instance, let's say you are an avid mountain biker. In the off-season, you could run a volunteer spinning class for underprivileged children in your community.

Giving is Living

We are hardwired to feel better after we've helped another person. It's why we were put on this earth. We are here to learn about unconditional love, and what better way to practice this lesson than volunteering?

Give From the Heart

Never underestimate the great tool you carry with you everywhere...your beautiful smile. It can touch the heart of an old friend, bring radiance to a stranger, and most importantly, it can change your whole outlook on life when you share it with yourself. Volunteering is as simple as sharing a smile. If you are too busy to schedule in some volunteer hours at the moment, surely you always have time to share your light.

CIRCLES

"The geometry of life is pretty simple— just encircle everyone with all your love."— Robert Clancy

❊

The sacred circle not only represents the entire universe, but also everything that surrounds your precious soul within it. In nature, circles are found in everything from the rings of a tree to the remarkable rings of Saturn, and in even our own planet's yearly journey around the sun. But are any of these circles perfect? It's been argued that the only perfect circles that exist are those in mathematics. Ah, but isn't that the beauty of it all? We are all born to be imperfect in the perfection of God's great math. We can never see the beautiful picture God has created for us, because we're always standing upon His blueprint.

You become what you surround yourself with, so why not encircle yourself with love? To transcend your circles, you must first visualize what is needed within them and what you need to release from them.

Recently, one of my life-long best friends succumbed to a rare form of cancer after a long hard-fought battle. We met in the first grade on our elementary playground, and from that moment on, we never questioned our friendship. We were simply friends in every sense of the word. Our souls knew it the instant we met.

The night before my wedding, we decided to go to the very playground where we met all those years ago. We talked for hours about our friendship, the funny moments, hard times, life, and marriage. It's a moment with him I will always cherish. We are so close that our children call each of us uncle, because our friendship became a brotherhood. Shortly after he passed away, I thought about what he brought to my life. I can sum it up in one word...*guidance*. All of your friends are guides, meant to be in your life at just the right moments.

After my friend was diagnosed, we agreed to be real with each other. Although we were very open in our discussions, we realized we had to talk real about the difficult subjects. It was the only way to successfully navigate the difficult times ahead. I'm so glad I had these moments with him. In the end, I had the precious opportunity to say everything to him I ever needed to. That's everything a friend is.

Your family and friends are your most precious circles that contain these special people—those who surround your heart with all their love. Although some friends may leave your circle over time, there are those who remain a part of your infinite loop forever, those who've always been there for you, those who've never doubted your friendship for a second. Those are your true friends.

These best friends are easy to sort out...they're the ones who've always been there to celebrate your every high point, and lifted you out of every low point; they've always carried your precious heart through it all.

If you take a circle and give it a twist in the middle, it becomes an infinity symbol. When your circle of life is not going so well, or even if it seems perfect, just give it a twist. This can lead to new and wonderful possibilities for your life!

Take a moment to reflect upon the infinite points of light

contained within the circles of your life. Never forget you are one of the brightest points on this endless continuum. Of all the circles in life, love is your greatest.

Enjoy your journey!

DECODES

Connect

One of your closest friends might be someone who you haven't spoken with in a while. Give them a call and let them know how much they mean to you. It's so easy to take for granted those who bring the most to your life.

Be Real

If you are holding back with a friend, determine why you feel that way. True friendship is unbreakable. If you are not true to your friend, how can you ever expect them to be with you?

Create a Positive Circle

You become what you surround yourself with. Better yet, you become whom you surround yourself with. It is perfectly fine to pull the weeds from your life. It's the only way the flowers have the room they need to bloom.

True Friends

True friends are with you thick and thin;

*They cry through your bad times, and celebrate
your wins.*

*You can always find them right there
by your side;*

Holding you up, rejoicing with pride.

This bond is forever, unbreakable and tough;

*For this friendship can only be called
one thing...love.*

FINAL DECODES

"Many scholars have debated the purpose of life. To me it's simple and it's always been about just one thing...love."— Robert Clancy

Love: Love is like a garden. The only things that will ever grow within it are the things you place there, nurture, and tenderly care for with all your heart. Some people claim love has never touched their life. This is like saying you've stood on the beach and never touched the ocean. With a little effort you could simply walk toward the waves or if you wait patiently enough, the tide will always bring the ocean to you. The sea of love is endless and it touches every shore.

Hope: The valleys of despair are always surrounded by mountains of hope; you just need a little faith to climb back to the top. You can never lose hope unless you choose to let go of it. Hold on!

Faith: When love becomes the air you breathe and hope becomes your sky, every faithful step you take in the valley of your fears will carry your precious soul from those shadows into the glorious light. May faith simply become belief.

Healing: Love is a healing hand that holds your heart high enough above the darkness to always see the light.

Forgiveness: Forgiving yourself allows you to let go of a past that's no longer relevant, create the future you've dreamed of, and more importantly, live fully in a present you so desperately deserve.

Smiles: One smile can warm a thousand hearts in the same way one person is capable of helping the lives of thousands. Combine the two, and you have an unstoppable force of kindness in the universe.

Gratitude: When you have a positive attitude that's filled with gratitude, all things on your life's latitude become possible.

Death: Death is never an end, but rather a chance for something new to begin.

Giving: A smile is the easiest way to volunteer. The first person you should share your beautiful smile with is yourself—each and every day!

Leadership: Great leaders may lead the charge, but quite often the greatest of those leaders also rescue the heart. Always lead others to a place of love and you will always end up in a place worth the journey. Leadership is much less about telling then it is about asking. You can never be truly decisive without knowing the complete problem you face.

Superheroes: All superheroes have a unique power or ability, but they also all have one in common...they never, ever give up on hope. We all have the capacity to be a superhero. In order to be one, you just have to find your unique power or ability and exploit it for the greater good of humanity. The cape and mask are optional accessories, but a kind heart is essential.

Wonderment: Rediscover your innocence and wonderment; set a play date with your inner child.

Silver Linings: Your destiny is not so much determined by what happens to you, but rather how you respond to life lessons. When you encounter setbacks, frustrations, or disappointments, the question is whether you've become a wiser, stronger, and better person. There is a plan for you and there is always a silver lining balancing every seemingly negative experience. You just need to recognize and acknowledge it. Dare to live life to the fullest, and embrace the challenges placed before you.

Supporting Others

"Volunteers may be the ones who give of their time, but they're always the ones who make time to give all their heart."— Robert Clancy

The author supports the New York East Hugh O'Brian Youth Leadership Seminar, which fosters youth leadership through community service and Junior Achievement of Northeastern New York, an organization that inspires and prepares young people for work readiness, entrepreneurship, and financial literacy through the use of experiential, hands-on programs.

Inspiring, Educational, Compassionate, Energizing, Enthusiastic, Motivating, Transforming, Long-Lasting, and Life-Changing

These are some of the words that students, schools, parents, alumni, volunteers, and supporters use to describe Hugh O'Brian Youth Leadership (HOBY).

Founded in 1958, HOBY's mission is to inspire and develop our global community of youth and volunteers to a life dedicated to leadership, service, and innovation. HOBY programs are conducted annually throughout the United States, serving local and international high school students.

The New York East Leadership Seminar provides youth in eastern New York a unique three-day motivational leadership training, service learning, and motivation-building experience. New York East HOBY also provides adults with opportunities to make a significant impact on the lives of youth by volunteering.

NYE Hugh O'Brian Youth Leadership Seminar
PO Box 14471, Albany, NY 12212-4471
www.hobynye.org

Explore the Power of JA

Junior Achievement is Northeastern New York's largest organization dedicated to educating students about issues relating to work readiness, entrepreneurship, and financial literacy through the use of experiential, hands-on programs. In partnership with the business and education communities, and through the support of community volunteers, JA brings the real world to students, opening their minds to their potential.

Junior Achievement of Northeastern New York, Inc.
8 Stanley Circle, Latham, NY 12110
phone: (518) 783-4336
www.janeny.org

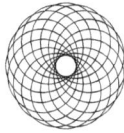

ABOUT THE AUTHOR

Robert Clancy is a gifted technology entrepreneur, acclaimed author, spiritual teacher, and inspirational speaker from New York. At age nineteen, Robert had a divine spiritual experience that greatly altered his life. In 2012 he started "Robert Clancy – Guide to the Soul" Facebook fan page (facebook. com/GuideToTheSoul) where he shares his divinely inspired thoughts, now followed by hundreds of thousands of people worldwide. Robert is also a regular contributor on Los Angeles KABC Radio's Late Night Health Radio show.

Through his passion for exceptional design & innovative technology, he co-founded Spiral Design Studio (SpiralDesign. com) more than 25 years ago to lead an award winning creative team in the evolution of major corporate brands, marketing & web development. Robert is a husband, father and 5th degree master black belt martial arts instructor. He is also a dedicated volunteer who completely embodies the spirit of service—a selfless commitment to helping others make a positive difference in the world.

As early as age six, Robert had immense compassion for humanity. He commits his life to assisting others, whether volunteering, helping them to succeed, or even just offering a friendly smile. Robert is a husband, father, and 5th Degree Master Black Belt martial arts instructor. Through many years of volunteer work, he's amassed a collection of awards and has served in leadership positions for Hugh O'Brian Youth Leadership (HOBY), Junior Achievement, the American Marketing Association, and the Graphic Artists Guild, among others.

Robert Clancy is a dedicated volunteer who completely embodies the spirit of service—a selfless commitment to helping others make a positive difference in the world.

Spiral Design Studio, LLC
135 Mohawk Street,
Cohoes NY 12047
ph: (518) 326-1135 • fx: (518) 326-2342
www.spiraldesign.com

More Guide to the Soul!

Do you have a compelling story about a kindred spirit,
a lesson in compassion, or a captivating view on volunteerism
that has changed your life? If so, I invite you to submit your
story to be considered for publication in the upcoming
follow up *Guide to the Soul* books and projects.

Stories may be up to fifteen hundred words and must be either
a lesson in compassion or a captivating story on volunteerism
that is uplifting and inspiring. You may submit your own
original piece, something you've read, or your favorite
inspirational quote.

To obtain a copy of the submission guidelines and submit
your story, please visit the Guide to the Soul website at www.
guidetothesoul.com or contact us at the address below.

We ensure that all original submissions are credited.

For submissions, guidelines, and more information:

Guide to the Soul Submissions
135 Mohawk Street
Cohoes, NY 12047
Phone: (518) 326-1135
Fax: (518) 326-2342

email: submissions@guidetothesoul.com
www.guidetothesoul.com

SPEAKING OPPORTUNITIES

●

Have the author speak at your next event!

Robert Clancy's compelling speaking engagements and seminars are now available for your company, non-profit, or organization!

In his signature keynote speeches, *Decoding a Masterful Life* and *Leadership from the Heart* Robert uses examples from his books, *Soul Cyphers* and *The Hitchhiker's Guide to the Soul*, to learn how to improve your leadership through a compassion for others. Gain a sense of renewed purpose and self-worth. Realize the importance of your connection to humanity and how it enhances your career and life—everyday. Discover the exceptional power of kindness and the unexpected opportunities it provides to those who dare to give.

For all inquiries please contact us at:

Guide to the Soul
135 Mohawk Street
Cohoes, NY 12047
Phone: (518) 326-1135

email: inquiries@guidetothesoul.com
www.guidetothesoul.com

Your Time to Shine

●

I would love to hear about from you about your life-changing volunteer experiences and your reaction to this book. If there was a particular story that added meaning to your life, please let me know how it affected you.

Do you have a compelling story about a kindred spirit, a lesson in compassion, or a captivating view on volunteerism that has changed your life? If so, I invite you to submit your story to be considered for publication in the future books and projects.

Please send your submissions to:

Guide to the Soul, LLC
135 Mohawk Street
Cohoes, NY 12047
Fax: (518) 326 2342

For complete submission guidelines and online submissions, visit the *Guide to the Soul* website at
www.guidetothesoul.com

Share on Facebook at *facebook.com/guidetothesoul*

I hope you enjoy reading this book and that it inspires you choose a life path of compassion, grace, healing, happincoo, peace, and unconditional love.

Why ask why, when you should simply ask why not.

www.ingramcontent.com/pod-product-compliance
Lightning Source LLC
Chambersburg PA
CBHW052034090426
42739CB00010B/1907